KATHLEEN CRUZIC, a registered nurse, has written several articles for magazines about health, child care, animals, and business. She has had many years of practical experience caring for handicapped people, both personally and professionally.

DISABLED? YES. DEFEATED? NO.

Resources for the Disabled and Their Families, Friends, and Therapists

KATHLEEN CRUZIC

A SPECTRUM BOOK

Prentice-Hall, Inc. Englewood Cliffs, New Jersey 07632

Library of Congress Cataloging in Publication Data

Cruzic, Kathleen.
   Disabled? yes, defeated? no.

   (A Spectrum Book)
   Bibliography: p.
   Includes index.
      1. Handicapped—Handbooks, manuals, etc.   2. Self-help
devices for the handicapped—Handbooks, manuals, etc.
   3. Handicapped—Services for—Handbooks, manuals, etc.
   4. Handicapped—Bibliography.   I. Title.
HV1568.C77   617   81-23533
ISBN 0-13-215681-4   AACR2
ISBN 0-13-215673-3 (pbk.)

This Spectrum Book is available to businesses and organizations at a special discount when ordered in large quantities. For information, contact Prentice-Hall, Inc., General Publishing Division, Special Sales, Englewood Cliffs, N. J. 07632.

© 1982 by Kathleen Cruzic. All rights reserved. No part of this book may be reproduced in any form or by any means without permission in writing from the publisher. Printed in the United States of America.

At the time of publication, most of the specific products mentioned in this book have been generally accepted by experts in the rehabilitation field. However, neither the author nor the publisher has been able to personally test every item listed in this book, so the reader is advised to make his or her own evaluations.

Editorial/production supervision by Frank Moorman
Cover design by Michael Freeland
Manufacturing buyer: Cathie Lenard

A SPECTRUM BOOK

10 9 8 7 6 5 4 3 2 1

ISBN 0-13-215681-4

ISBN 0-13-215673-3 {pbk.}

PRENTICE-HALL INTERNATIONAL, INC., *London*
PRENTICE-HALL OF AUSTRALIA PTY. LIMITED, *Sydney*
PRENTICE-HALL CANADA INC., *Toronto*
PRENTICE-HALL INDIA PRIVATE LIMITED, *New Delhi*
PRENTICE-HALL JAPAN, INC., *Tokyo*
PRENTICE-HALL OF SOUTHEAST ASIA PTE. LTD., *Singapore*
WHITEHALL BOOKS LIMITED, *Wellington, New Zealand*

CONTENTS

What This Book Will Do for You

Introduction

STRICTLY FOR COMFORT, 1
Ways to Relieve Pressure, 1   Stretch Gloves for Arthritic Hands, 2   Supports While Lying in Bed, 3   Tips for Comfort, 4   Sources for Obtaining Products, 4

AIDS TO DAILY LIVING, 7
Bathing, 8   Oral Hygiene, 8   Grooming, 9   Dressing, 10   Eating and Drinking, 11   Additional Tips, 12   Helpful Booklets, 13   Sources for Obtaining Products, 13

HOW'S YOUR FASHION IMAGE?, 20
Sources for Obtaining Clothes, 20   Mastectomy Clothes and Products, 38   Alterations and Sewing, 42   Tips for Altering Clothes, 46   Sewing Hints, 47   Brighten Your Wheelchair, Cane, or Crutches, 48   Clothing Consultants, 49   Choice of Clothing, 49   Caring for Your Clothes, 51

SHORTCUTS TO HOUSEWORK, 53
Organizing Your Work, 53   Substitutes for Cleaning Tools, 54   Housekeeping Hints, 56   Laundry Tips, 60   List of Publications, 60   List of Products Available, 61

WHEN YOU ARE THE COOK IN THE KITCHEN, 62
Adaptions You Can Make, 62   Choosing Your Appliances, 63   Handy Utensils and Tools, 64   Planning the Menu, 65   Getting the Meal on the Table, 65   Clean-up Chores, 66   Cooking Tips, 67   Kitchen Hints, 70   Helpful Books, 72   Products Available, 74

THE GATES OF LEARNING ARE OPEN WIDE, 76
Getting Your High School Diploma, 76   Adult Education Programs, 77   The Two-Year College, 78   The Four-Year College, 80   Financial Assistance, 81   TV Courses for Credit, 83   Vocational Training, 84   Corporate Training Programs, 84   Home Study or Correspondence Courses, 85

TRY ON A NEW CAREER, 89
Handicapped People with Outstanding Careers, 89   Other Examples of Occupations, 95   A Directory of Federal and State Programs, 95

HELP FROM THE PRINTED PAGE, 97
Booklets, 97   Magazines, 99   Newspapers, 100   Newsletters, 100   Handicapped Children, 101   Practical Help for the Handicapped, 102   Sex and the Handicapped, 106   Inspirational and Motivational Books, 107   Available in Large Print, 114   Braille or Talking Books, 115   Homebound Book Service, 115   Library Outreach Service, 116   Book Cassettes to Rent, 116

ORGANIZATIONS THAT OFFER HELP, 117

STRETCHING YOUR DOLLARS, 128
Social Security Disability, 128   Public Assistance, 128   Supplemental Security Income, 129   Voluntary Organizations, 129   Special Income Tax Deductions, 129   Veteran's Benefits, 130   Small Business Loans, 131   Housing Alternatives, 131   Mobile Homes, 132   Insurance, 132   Mail-Order Shopping, 133   Mail-Order Houses, 133   Saving Money, 136

THOSE FARAWAY PLACES, 138
Travel Agencies, 138   Special Preparations, 140   Tips for Packing, 140   Medical Preparations, 141   Medical Help When Traveling, 142   Good Health in Four Languages, 142   When You Plan to Fly, 143   Car Rentals, 146   When You Go by Train, 147   Travel by Bus, 148   Travel by Car, 149

Hotel-Motel Guides, 150   Travel Books and Pamphlets, 151
Gadgets for Gadabouts, 153

YOU CAN RIDE A HOBBY HORSE, 155

Reading or Listening to Books, 155   Collecting, 156   Music, 157
Crafts, 157   Needlework, 159   Gardening, 160   Bird
Watching or Feeding, 160   Photography, 161   Ham Radio, CB,
and Shortwave, 162   Pen Pal or Tape Pal Clubs, 163   Art as a
Hobby or Career, 164   Writing Can Be Rewarding, 164
Bringing Joy to Others, 165

TIME OUT FOR PLAY, 166

Sports, 166   Camping, 179   Fishing, 180   Hunting and
Shooting, 180   Games and Puzzles, 181   Sightseeing, 181
Cultural Activities, 183   Special Programs, 184   Product
Listing and Sources, 184

PRODUCTS FOR THE HANDICAPPED, 187

Aids to Daily Living, 187   Mobility, 189   Transportation, 190
Communication, 192   Miscellaneous, 194   Catalogs, 194

DON'T OVERLOOK THE SPIRITUAL, 197

The Bible, 197   Churches, 198   Radio Programs, 199   TV
Programs, 200   Bible Study Groups, 200   Prayer by
Telephone, 200   Inspirational Literature, 200   Christian
Volunteer Groups, 201   Accessible Churches, 202

WHAT COMMUNITIES ARE DOING, 203

Transportation, 203   Public Buildings, 205   Officials Spend a
Day in a Wheelchair, 206   Curb Cuts and Parking, 206   Radio
and TV Programs, 207   Service Centers, 207   Housing, 208

WHAT THIS BOOK CAN DO FOR YOU

Disabled? Yes. Defeated? NO. is packed with information to help you lead a richer, more productive life no matter what your disability. It will help with a short-term problem such as a sprained ankle, a broken arm, a minor back problem, or a more serious long-term condition.

Do you want to increase your activities, find a hobby, travel, learn about new products, or consider a new career? This book will give answers to those questions and many more.

You, the reader, may be the disabled individual, a member of the family, a friend, or one of the professionals in the health field—the doctor, nurse, physiotherapist, occupational therapist, or teacher.

This is a resource guide you will refer to repeatedly. For example, here are seven immediate results you can acheive.

1. You will be spared hours of research delving into books, magazines, pamphlets, and catalogs, along with hours of interviewing people for pertinent information. It's all here in one easy-to-read book.
2. You can start using tips for saving time in dressing, grooming, doing housework, and performing many other activities.
3. You will find new sources for products, clothing, and equipment which will help you select the best product for the job as well as allow you to compare price and quality.

4. You can save money by learning to adapt items found in the home or at the nearest department store or toy counter. Many times you can find a lightweight or inexpensive substitute for a more expensive product.
5. You will find lots of ideas for obtaining further information such as lists of books and publications you may want to explore. These are applicable to the disabled individual, to his family, or to those working with him.
6. You will get encouragement and inspiration to try for bigger goals. The nurse, teacher, or therapist can find ways to reinforce these goals for his or her patient.
7. There are suggestions for getting more fun and enjoyment out of living which can be used by the disabled individual and by anyone living or working with him or her.

INTRODUCTION

The need for this type of book first became apparent when I needed to help my mother remain as active as possible while she was disabled with osteoarthritis. In caring for her at home, we encountered many problems: Where do you find specially designed clothing with substitutes for unmanageable buttons and zippers? Is there a device for putting on stockings when you can't bend over? If these products are available, how do you locate them, and do you have more than one choice?

As a nurse, I thought finding the answers to these and other questions would be easy. But how wrong I was! It sometimes took many hours to find the answer to a single question. Because I found this search so long and so frustrating, I wanted to save others from this experience, and thus the idea for this book was born. When I subsequently developed rheumatoid arthritis, with its ever increasing problems of painful, swollen joints and often limited motion, I intensified my search for information.

For some time my goal had been to develop a retirement career with a different kind of challenge from nursing, so I studied writing in the evening and during weekend classes while continuing to work full time. Although I was forced into retirement earlier than expected by the rheumatoid arthritis, I had firsthand experience in coping with a painful, chronic, and disabling disease, and I was already writing and selling magazine and newspaper articles. Thus I felt I had the necessary background to write this book. As the book began to take shape and I talked with doctors, other nurses, and patients, I realized the book could benefit a wide range of individuals.

From the experience with my mother, I knew how much families, as well as patients, needed this kind of information. Since my nursing experience included years of patient care, followed by many years of nursing administration and teaching, I knew I was qualified to include the health care professional as well as the disabled individual.

Dedication

Dedicated with love and gratitude
to all my friends who helped transform
this book from dream to reality.

chapter one
STRICTLY FOR COMFORT

Personal comfort is vitally important to everyone. A disabling illness or injury is bad enough without having to put up with nagging discomforts that can be eliminated. Your personal comfort is important whether you have a broken leg that will heal in a few weeks or a chronic condition that requires long-term consideration.

The following suggestions and tips offer many ideas you may be able to adapt to your own situation. Some items can be made at home or bought at department stores, while others can be ordered from more specialized sources. At the end of the chapter you will find a wide variety of products and sources listed along with names and addresses.

Ways to Relieve Pressure

SPONGE RUBBER
Sponge rubber comes in different sizes and thicknesses and it can be carved into whatever you need, such as foot or heel pads, arm rests, and padding for use with braces, casts, crutches, and other orthopedic appliances.

One man tells how uncomfortable he was spending twelve to sixteen hours a day in his wheelchair and not finding a cushion that adequately relieved the bony protuberances he sat on. He solved the problem by scooping out an oval area about six inches by twelve inches in a four-inch-thick sponge rubber cushion. This placed the main pressure on his hip bones and allowed him to sit up to sixteen hours daily in relative comfort without fear of decubitus pressure sores.

If you prefer to buy these products rather than make them, there is a list of sources at the end of the chapter.

VERSATILE TAILOR-MADE PILLOWS

One of the most versatile gadgets for comfort is a small pillow you can make at home. Place two washcloths together and stitch around three and one half sides. Then turn them inside out so the seams are hidden and stuff with nylon hose or pantyhose cut in pieces. Close remaining opening by hand so the stitching doesn't show, and you have a machine-washable pillow. Use bright colors and trim with fringe made from washable yarn.

This pillow is just the right size to protect a painful elbow or shoulder from resting against the side rails of a hospital bed or wheelchair, to take the pressure off a painful joint when lying in bed, to protect a painful arm, knee, or foot from pressure when sitting in a wheelchair, to tuck under the edge of a cast, or to provide a small head pillow when a regular one is too big. Once you have one of these small pillows, you will find so many uses for it, you may wonder how you ever did without it.

Stretch Gloves for Arthritic Hands

Wearing stretch gloves at night has brought comfort to many arthritis sufferers. They experience greatly reduced morning pain and stiffness and reduced joint swelling. Some have noted an increased grip strength. How the gloves work is not clear but symptoms are usually reduced in the first two or three days. This innovation has helped some people sleep through the night for the first time in several years. A combination of spandex and nylon seems to be the most comfortable, although nylon knit gloves can also be worn.

Dr. George E. Ehrlich, director of the Arthritis Clinic at Albert Einstein Medical Center, Philadelphia, conducted an experiment with a group of his patients, after which several of them told him how much the stretch gloves helped. He found that all but three patients showed marked relief when they kept the gloves on overnight. It worked for patients with osteo-arthritis, rheumatoid arthritis, plus some other painful conditions.

These gloves are now available at most drug and department stores. If you can't find them there, try the surgical supply outlets. Men who need larger sizes may have some difficulty finding them, but perhaps writing to the manufacturer would help.

Supports while Lying in Bed

Should you wish instructions for making any of the following, you can obtain them in *Home Nursing Textbook* put out by the American National Red Cross and available at your public library.

BACKRESTS
Several varieties of backrests, such as a rattan car seat, a triangular pillow, or a contoured one with armrests can be purchased. Or, if you prefer, you can improvise one from a cardboard box. It should be twenty-four by twenty-three by twenty-eight inches with the cover flaps attached. It can be covered with a bath towel or other material.

FOOT SUPPORTS
A foot support allowing one foot or both to maintain a normal position when lying on one's back or sitting in bed can also be made from a cardboard box if you don't want to buy one. This will help prevent foot drop and other deformities and keep the weight of bed clothes off the feet.

BED CRADLES
To keep bed clothes off an injured leg or other part of the body, you can buy or rent a bed cradle, or improvise one from a large wooden box, crate, or cardboard carton. This keeps the bed clothes off the desired part of the body and yet gives freedom to move around or sleep in a comfortable position.

BED BLOCKS

If the bed is too low for getting on or off easily, bed blocks under the legs will give extra height. Wooden blocks with a center indentation carved out or molding glued around the edges to keep the bed from slipping off are two suggestions. If you take the casters off so the bed won't slide, cinder or cement blocks can be used instead.

Additional Tips for Comfort

1. To make turning in bed easier, make a satin half sheet that goes across the bed and over the bottom sheet. Buy enough satin for the width of your bed. Sew a strip of terrycloth on both ends of the satin to tuck under the mattress. The rough terrycloth keeps the satin from slipping out of place.

2. Baby blankets are just the right size for lap robes for wheelchair patients; they are not too heavy and are easily laundered. They come in a wide variety of colors and designs.

3. One wheelchair occupant solved the problem of keeping her legs warm on cold windy days by making a cover out of wool in the shape of a sack and lined with a smooth material. This slips over the legs and each side ties to the top of the arms of the wheelchair.

4. Large thermal mugs protect hands from excessive heat and cold, have a larger holding area and eliminate the need to grip tightly.

5. For extra warmth for painful elbows and knees, cut the feet off a pair of men's heavy work socks and slip the tops over the painful joints. These can be hidden by a long-sleeved blouse or shirt or worn under a pant suit or slacks.

6. An oriental backscratcher can be very useful for scratching your head, ear, or nose if you don't have full use of your arms. It's also great for scratching under the edges of casts or for retrieving bits of loose plaster that sometimes get caught under it. It is useful in pulling things toward you with the curved end. It's lightweight, inexpensive, and most oriental gift shops carry them.

Sources for Obtaining Products

The following list contains items you may wish to purchase. Most companies carry many more items than are listed but this will give you some idea of what is available.

1. Dynamic Systems, Inc., Leicester, N.C. 28748
   A. Sun Mate cushion—A body sensitive cushion. Comes in different sizes, in soft, medium, or firm.
2. Everest and Jennings, Inc., 1803 Pontius Avenue, Los Angeles, Calif. 90025
   A. Foam rubber cushions—Cloth or leatherette covered cushions for seat or back. Come in various sizes.
3. Fashion Able, Rocky Hill, N.J. 08553
   A. Rest cushion—Each side inflates separately. Contact-free center. Fights fatigue and soreness. Makes car travel less tiring.
   B. Elbow and heel protectors—Soft cushioned comfort. Decreases irritation of sensitive skin. Helps prevent decubitus ulcers. Porous for air circulation. Outer surface slides easily over sheets. Permits maximum movement and position change.
   C. Arm cushion—Unique design cradles sensitive, sore arm. Soothes the discomfort of arthritis. Adjustable for height and softness. Vinyl, slippered cover, washable.
   D. Knee warmers—Can be worn under or over stockings.
4. Jobst Institute, Inc., P.O. Box 653, Toledo, Ohio 43694
   A. Hydro-Float wheelchair pads, mattresses, commode seats, and other products. (Check your local orthopedic supplier.)
5. Ken McRight Supplies, Inc., 7456 South Oswego, Tulsa, Okla. 74136
   A. Air cushions for preventing decubiti.
6. Personal Care Products Division, 3M Company, 3M Center #223–1N, Saint Paul, Minn. 55101
   A. Cold/hot Pack—Serves as ice pack when cold, hot pack when heated in water.
   B. Self-adhering foam pad—Flexible, may be cut or molded.
   C. Waterproof first-aid tape.
   D. Action Tape—Stretches as you move for hard-to-bandage places. Good for holding in place a pad, a splint, or dressing.
7. Posey Company, 5635 Peck Road, Arcadia, Calif. 91006
   A. Heel protector—Has hook and eye fasteners for easy application and sure fit.
   B. Elbow protector—Helps eliminate pressure sores and friction burns.
   C. Foot-Guard with T Bar Stabilizer—Simultaneously keeps weight of bedding off foot and helps prevent foot drop and foot rotation.
   D. Paraplegic wheelchair belt.
   E. Many other products such as safety vests, wheelchair accessories, and orthopedic and pediatric products.

8. Rehabilitation Equipment and Supply, 1823 West Moss Avenue, Peoria, Ill. 61606
   A. Spenco Gel cushion—Designed especially for wheelchair patients to eliminate decubitus ulcers and to provide relief from rectal and prostate tenderness in any type seat.
   B. Skin Care bed pad—Size—17 by 17 inches.
   C. Foot and heel protectors with liners.

9. Sears Roebuck and Company—Sears publishes a special catalog called CATALOG OF HOME HEALTH CARE. For information call or write the Sears store nearest you. For supplying heat to sore muscles or joints, they offer the following:
   A. Arthro muff—Helps relieve pain of aching joints and muscles. Can be used with moist or dry heat. For elbows, wrists, knees, ankles, and feet. Three settings—low, medium, and high.
   B. Wrap-around heat bandage—Allows you to wrap around almost any part of your body. Four ties allow you to secure bandage to body. Three settings—low, medium, and high.
   C. Grab bars and bath and shower benches, plus many other bathing and toilet aids such as elevated toilet seats.

Don't overlook the ordinary gift catalogs for items of personal comfort. Miles Kimball, Walter Drake, Montgomery Ward, J. C. Penney, and others often have items you need at lower prices than other sources.

If you want to rent larger items such as bed cradles, be sure to shop around. Some rental firms offer reasonable rates, whereas others are outrageously expensive.

chapter two
AIDS TO DAILY LIVING

This chapter covers some ideas and suggestions to make the routines of daily living easier. However, these are not intended to cover all the basic aids to daily living (ADL) found in standard ADL books or learned in the hospital.

Sometimes small problems are overlooked but they are nonetheless vexing. For example, trying to hold on to the soap in the shower may seem trivial, but if you have only the use of one hand and need that for steadying yourself, or if you can't bend over to pick up the soap if you drop it, the problem becomes an important one. So these tips contributed by patients and friends may be helpful to you.

The list of products and their sources includes many standard ADL devices and some that may be new to you. These items are listed to help you find the ones best suited to your individual needs. The variety of listings will also give you an opportunity to compare prices.

Most of these catalogs and books contain many other products to consider. This list is merely a sampling selected to give an idea of what is available.

Bathing

1. To keep from slipping when grasping the edge of the bathtub with wet hands, take some nonskid flowers or strips (the kind used on the bottom of the tub) and put them on the edges of the tub.

2. One way to keep soap from dropping out of reach is to tie a bar of soap in the toe of an old nylon stocking. Make a slipknot at the other end to slip over the wrist. Or make a soap on a rope to hang around your neck. Take an open-weave dishcloth, hem the top and insert cotton cording long enough to close the edges and to hang around your neck.

3. One method of anchoring a towel for hand use in bathroom or kitchen is to wrap one end around the towel bar and make a knot so the towel won't fall to the floor. It could also be pinned, held with Velcro strips, or tapes sewn on for ties.

4. A bath mitt made from terry toweling is useful for bathing when a person has the use of only one hand.

5. Some stores carry vinyl slipover shower hoods without fasteners that are handy for the person who can't manage the regular elasticized shower cap. Some styles of rain bonnets can also serve as shower caps.

6. Those who have trouble drying their backs with a regular bath towel can make their own from toweling cut and hemmed to the desired length with large tape loops sewn on each end. Only slight shoulder and elbow movement is needed. Or how about a large beach towel as a wrap around to dry all over?

Oral Hygiene

1. If an unsteady hand makes brushing your teeth a problem, try doing it a different way. Lean your elbow against the bathroom washbowl and, instead of moving your hand back and forth, move your head back and forth.

2. Consider a cordless electric toothbrush for easier handling and maneuverability.

3. For those who have dentures and have the use of only one hand, you can clean them with a brush secured to the wash basin with suction cups. The dentures can be held with one hand and

rubbed against the brush. Or ask the dentist or druggist about commercial denture soaking solutions that are available.

Grooming

1. Shaving
    a. Choose shaving cream in a pressurized can to eliminate mixing lather.
    b. A shaving brush can be held in an extension clamp for anyone having the use of only one hand. These clamps are available from chemical and scientific supply companies.
    c. For the person who prefers an electric razor, there are several lightweight battery-operated models such as Norelco and Schick for men, Lady Remington and others for women.
2. Make-up
    a. If small objects are difficult to grasp, a lipstick or mascara tube can be made thicker with a piece of foam rubber or several layers of tape.
    b. A wooden stick with a spring clothespin attached to the end can hold a powder puff.
3. Cologne and perfume—Cologne, perfume, and other cosmetics in lightweight spray containers may be easier to handle than bottles or jars. Purse-size travel or sample containers are often a good choice.
4. Deodorants—Find a personally preferred brand that works best, then choose the type of container easiest to handle—roll-on, stick, cream, or spray-on.
5. Hair care
    a. Use shampoo in a plastic bottle, which is lighter to handle and won't break if dropped. If the kind preferred comes in a glass container, transfer it to an empty plastic soap or detergent bottle.
    b. Dry shampoos can keep hair oil-free and fluffy between regular shampoos.
    c. Consider the attractive inexpensive wigs now available. If possible, get two or three for variety to enjoy more than one style or color. They are great for anyone who has difficulty keeping their hair attractively styled.
    d. For those who have weak or nonexistent deltoids, and can't raise their arms to comb or brush their hair, here is a useful homemade gadget. Take a piece of doweling (about twelve inches long) and a rattailed comb or small brush with a handle, and attach together at one end with a sturdy tape at about a fifteen degree angle.

Dressing

1. Putting on a bra—Underwear is hard for some women to put on. Those who cannot fasten a bra behind them may find that doing it in front is the answer. I put mine on backward, then twist it around the proper way and get my arms under the straps. For those who must work with one hand, make a fastener of Velcro. Or you may prefer to buy a front closing bra.

2. Slips—A half slip is easier than a regular slip for many women using crutches or wheelchairs. It can be either pulled over the head or up from the feet—just be sure the elasticized waistband is large enough to slip over the hips without difficulty. Or make a wrap-around half slip using Velcro fasteners or tailor hooks.

3. Substitutes for buttons and zippers—One answer for those who cannot manage buttons is Velcro strips sewn into the closing of a blouse, skirt, dress, trousers, or shirt instead of buttons and zippers. Velcro also comes in an iron-on variety. It comes in neutral colors such as white, black, or beige and is sold by the yard at fabric shops and variety stores.

There is also a Talon Zephyr slide fastener available where sewing supplies are stocked. This fastener has no teeth and can't catch either material or skin.

4. Sport shirts and Levi's—For those who like to wear sport shirts but can't button them, one solution is to sew the buttonholes closed and then sew the buttons over the old slits. Then sew Velcro tape down the front for opening and closing.

5. Zippers—There are chain zipper pulls available at notion or department stores, or you can attach a long piece of heavy sewing thread or yarn in the head of the zipper and knot the ends of the thread together to make a pull. After pulling up the back zipper, tuck the thread inside the dress. Match the thread or yarn to the dress and it will remain almost invisible.

6. Putting on socks and trousers—(Useful for those with limited hip and/or knee flexion.) One man fashioned his own gadget for putting on socks and trousers. He used two dowel rods (sections of broom handle would do) with eyehooks inserted in one end of each dowel. He then attached small cloth loops (twill tape is

a good choice) to the top sides of each sock. By holding a dowel in each hand he can hook the tabs on his socks and draw them on. The length of the dowel depends on the amount of reach needed.

He grasps his trousers by hooking either the inside waistband or the belt loops. Utilizing the "hook sticks," both legs are placed in the trousers and the trousers are then pulled within hand reach to finish the job. It only takes a matter of seconds to complete the process.

There is no reason why, with a little ingenuity, the same gadget can't be adapted to women's panties, girdles, and pantsuits.

7. Shoes—Slip-on styles are exasperating to wear as they are inclined to fall off when transferring to or from a wheelchair. Buckled or tied shoes are more likely to stay on. When going somewhere and wearing a slip-on style, just carry the shoes along to your destination and then put them on.

Eating and Drinking

1. Drive two or three *aluminum* nails through the bottom of a cutting board so the points stick up about two inches, to spear meat for slicing, toast for buttering, potatoes for peeling, etc. This gadget works well for anyone with limited arm or hand use. Note: It is important to use aluminum nails because they don't rust.

2. A bread holder can also be made by mounting a right-angled ledge on one corner of a breadboard. This will hold the bread in place while buttering it.

3. Another idea is to drive *aluminum* nails through the bottom of a wooden bowl. One stroke patient who loves grapefruit says this allows her to handle it with her one good arm.

4. Baby plates which hold hot water help keep food warm for patients who are slow in feeding themselves.

5. Extra long drinking straws can be fashioned from plastic tubing that can be cut to any length desired. Inserted in a pitcher of ice water or juice, it can be more easily reached from bed or wheelchair.

6. If a glass tumbler is hard to hold because of a weak grasp or poor coordination, there are attractive plastic ones that aren't as

slippery at department, drug, or variety stores and also from mail-order firms.

7. If more help is needed, decorate glasses with the same nonskid safety stickers used on bathtubs. They are good for cups, bowls, and other dishes as well.

8. For holding onto glasses at a party or restaurant, one idea is to keep a stretch knit coaster (the kind that fits over the bottom of a glass) with you at these occasions.

9. When a nonspillable drinking container is needed for water or other cold liquid, one can be fashioned from any plastic food carton such as a refrigerator storage container, margarine tub, or whatever, by making a hole in the lid for a straw. A couple of ice cubes or some crushed ice keeps it cold.

Additional Tips

1. A kitchen-type turntable or lazy susan makes many items reachable on bedside table, dresser, desk, or other work areas.

2. One woman finds a travel ironing board ideal as a bed-to-chair board. A teflon-coated cover facilitates sliding. It is strong and thin but not heavy.

3. Holding onto a phone requires more strength than some people have. To carry on conversations with ease, one helpful aid is a shoulder phone rest which enables a person to talk on the phone without hanging onto it every minute. It can be bought through various mail-order catalogs or at a local office supply store.

When lifting the telephone is difficult or impossible, some answering devices work by tripping a small switch, allowing the person to both listen and speak without lifting the handpiece at all. Check with the telephone company or an electronic supply house to find out what's available.

4. Another use for Velcro is to fasten down small radios and other appliances. It holds without marring tables and other furniture.

5. Soap holders with tiny suction cups all over provide an inexpensive means of holding things in place without sliding. Place

Aids To Daily Living

them underneath a mixing bowl, a plate or cereal bowl, a make-up compact, and other items.

6. Nylon or satin sheets can ease moving about in bed or are just great if you have to be moved or turned.

7. Anyone who has trouble gripping eating utensils, pens, and pencils, can enlarge the grip on these and other slender items by using foam or plastic cylinders from hair curlers.

8. A bicycle basket fastened to the front bar of a walker is convenient for carrying things.

9. For those who have trouble reading paperback books because the pages won't lie flat, you can have a print shop remove the original binding and replace it with a spiral binding made of plastic. Most well-equipped print shops can do the job.

Helpful Booklets

1. ART OF MAKE-UP FOR THE VISUALLY HANDICAPPED
   Lighthouse, Braille Department, 111 East 59th Street, New York, N.Y. 10022—A twenty-four-page booklet available for a small charge.
2. TOOTH BRUSHING AND FLOSSING and HELPING HANDICAPPED PERSONS CLEAN THEIR TEETH
   Easter Seal Society, 2023 West Ogden Avenue, Chicago, Ill. 60612—Both booklets available for a small charge.
3. MEALTIME MANUAL FOR THE AGED AND HANDICAPPED
   Rehabilitation Medicine, New York University Medical Center, 400 East 34th Street, New York, N.Y. 10016—Contains hints for the elderly, and the homemaker with one hand, arthritis, weakness of upper extremities, poor or no coordination, limited vision, and much more.

Sources for Obtaining Products

1. ADL CATALOG
   Cleo Living Aids, 3957 Mayfield Road, Cleveland, Ohio 44121 (Toll-free telephone number—800-321-0595)
   A. Push-button folding commode—Folds flat for storage or transportation.
   B. Raised seat attachment—The added four-inch height is enough to allow you to use facility with minimum effort. Fits any standard toilet.
   C. Safety tub rail—Clamps securely on any tub. Provides needed grip for security.

D. Safety bathtub grip—Banishes fear of falling, portable.
E. Bathtub safety rails—Adjustable, fits over side of tub.
F. Little Octopus—Powerful suction cups hold to any surface. Holds soap and also dishes firmly. Comes in various colors.
G. Zipper shoe fastener—Permits shoes to be put on and taken off without undoing laces. Zips open and closed. For five- or six-eyelet shoes. Black or brown.
H. Utility stick combination—Consists of a rod of lightweight aluminum tubing about two feet long. Has a loop holder on one end. At other end several devices are provided and can be used interchangeably to hold bath sponge, comb, reaching hook, shoe horn, magnet. For patients whose activities are limited either by weakness or loss of range of motion.

2. Better Sleep, Inc., New Providence, N.J. 07974
    A. Twin-rest seat cushion—Unlike embarrassing "ring cushions" it avoids side rocking and maintains your balance because each side inflates separately with contact-free center space.
    B. Foam padded back rest
    C. Crescent air pillow
    D. Comfort arm cushion

3. E. F. Brewer Company, 13901 Main Street, Menomonee Falls, Wis. 53051
    A. Bathroom safety needs

4. Century Home Health Care, P.O. Box 57, Healdsburgh, Calif. 95448
    A. Century bathing systems
    B. Patient transfer systems

5. Chesebrough-Ponds, Inc., Hospital Products Division, Greenwich, Conn. 06830
    A. Uri-Drain—A male urinary-control system

6. Conair Corporation, 11 Executive Avenue, Edison, N.J. 08817, or 2 North 59th Avenue, Phoenix, Ariz. 85043
    A. Illuminated Make-up Mirror, curling iron, hair dryers. (Many of these products may be found in drug or department stores.)

7. Walter Drake and Sons, 3058 Drake Building, Colorado Springs, Colo. 80940
    A. Toothpaste dispenser—Gives you toothpaste with the push of a button. Self-stick mounting; dispenser lifts off bracket for cleaning. Fits all tubes.
    B. Shower soap dish—Cradle shaped dish instantly attaches to shower wall, also ideal next to washbasin or kitchen sink.
    C. Bathtub safety rail—Fits over side of most tubs. Supports over 300 pounds. Rustproof, chrome-plated heavy steel tubing.
    D. Bathtub seat—Bathe in safety and comfort—great for foot baths, shampoos, sit-down showers, aids convalescents and elderly people. Fits any tub.

E. Johnny slip-on rack—Just hang rack over edge of tank. Holds books, magazines, etc.
F. Shampoo tray—Beauty shop comfort at home. Especially good for washing children's hair. Puts end to splashed floors and wet clothes. Fits any sink. Plastic, 13 inches long.
G. No-stoop tub scrubber—Long 26-inch handle lets you clean bathtubs standing up. Wonderful to clean hard-to-reach tile walls, showers. Chrome-plated.
H. Toe caps—Relieve sore toes. Shaped caps fit over toes to prevent irritating shoe pressure on sore toes, and discomfort of ingrown nails. Cups are washable. Set of two will fit all size toes.

8. Eaton E-Z Bath Company, Box 712, Garden City, Kans. 67845
   A. Bath lift for getting in and out of the bathtub.
9. Everest and Jennings, Inc., 1803 Pontius Avenue, Los Angeles, Calif. 90025
   A. Bath and safety aids.
   B. Walkers and other walking aids.
10. Fashion Able, Rocky Hill, N.J. 08553
    A. Suction hand brush—One-hand scrubbing equipment. Fine for dentures, great for cleaning vegetables, silverware, dishes. Nylon bristles in durable plastic. Two nonslip suction cups. Size: 1 by ½ by 4 inches.
    B. Telescope cane—Adjusts from 30 to 38 inches. Friction lock will not slip or be accidentally dislodged. Telescopes to 23 inches for storage. Comfortable rubber handle, heavy-duty sure-grip tip. Bright anodized aluminum.
    C. Folding adjustable walker—Safety device locks it in open position. Height adjusts easily: 32 to 38 inches. Folds for storage or travel. Rigid construction of anodized aluminum; chrome steel cross brace.
    D. Portable raised seat for toilet—Solid plastic seat, four sturdy supports with bumpers. Raises seat four inches.
    E. Stocking pull-on—Gather stocking over soft flexible form, attach fasteners, insert foot, pull up straps; 32 inches.
    F. No-bend shoe off—Insert heel into notch and pull up while holding the unit with other foot. Broad base, won't tip. Nonskid surface. Size: 6½ by 11½ inches long.
    G. Round-the-neck mirror—Leaves both hands free. Tilts, raises to any angle. Good for rear view, 6-inch mirror, one side magnifies, 11-inch arm.
11. Gerber Family Health Care, Gerber Products Company, 445 State Street, Fremont, Mich. 49412
    A. DRIpride—A convenient easy-to-use method to manage incontinency for individuals at home.
12. Ted Hoyer and Company, Inc., 2222 Minnesota Street, Oshkosh, Wis. 54901

A. Lifts for placing patient in tub and for other uses such as bed to wheelchair or into car.
13. Independence Factory, P.O. Box 597, Middleton, Ohio 45042
   A. Products for personal grooming
      a. Enlarged handle comb
      b. Extended handle hair brush
      c. Button aid
      d. Hair stick
      e. Extended nail clippers
      f. Faucet handle turner
14. Lumex, Inc., 100 Spence Street, Bay Shore, N.Y. 11706
   A. Health care equipment for hospital, nursing home, or home care—walkers, canes, crutches, bathroom products, commodes, elevated toilet seat devices, and grab bars.
15. Maddak, Inc., Pequannock, N.J. 07440
   A. Plastic utensil hand clip—Spring-action clip fits the hand and holds a spoon or fork securely. An excellent eating aid for persons having difficulty in grasping and holding small utensils.
   B. Three-function eating utensil—A stainless steel combined knife-fork-spoon to assist persons having limited hand function.
   C. Food bumper—This snap-on food bumper is a curved rail designed to keep food from sliding off the plate. Fits plates 9 to 11 inches in diameter.
   D. Tube holder and magnetic soap holder—A sanitary and convenient method of storing toothpaste, creams, hair dressings, medications, or soap. Keeps soap within reach and easier to grasp by persons with difficulty grasping.
   E. Long handled comb—Polished, rigid, alloy metal comb mounted on a lightweight aluminum angled handle with wood grip. Handle is 21 inches long; comb is 4 inches long.
   F. Nail brush with suction cups and nail file—Nylon bristle brush, size 3¾ by 1½ inches, is mounted on two suction cups.
   G. Nail scissors—Nickel-plated with plastic handle that automatically opens the scissors when squeeze pressure is released.
16. Miles Kimball Company, 41 West 8th Avenue, Oshkosh, Wis. 54901
   A. Nylon hosiery wash case—Put hose or delicate hand washables in case and send through washer.
   B. Shower caddy—Holds everything so you can shower in comfort. Caddy snaps into place on pipe behind all shower heads.
   C. Austrian backscrubber and massager—Canvas strap, size 4½ by 29 inches, has sheared sisal bristles that scrub gently and stimulate circulation.
   D. Magnetic easy reach—Extend reach by 27 inches. Slip-proof grips. Magnetic tips retrieve pins, paper clips, and other small objects. Also holds a sponge for quick mop-ups.

Aids To Daily Living

17. G.E. Miller, Inc., 484 South Broadway, Yonkers, N.Y. 10705
    A. Flex-O-Lace elastic shoe laces—Fit all oxfords, and come in black, brown, and white.
    B. Zip-Up shoe laces—This unique lacing device will enable a person to close his shoe laces with one hand.
    C. Utility holder—Plastic holder with Velcro for firm, adjustable attachment. Holds spoon or fork.
    D. Magic soaper—Holds soap inside sponge of soft natural rubber. Extra long 17-inch plastic handle.
    E. Extension spoon and fork—A device to aid those with limited motion in arms and shoulders.
    F. Three-purpose mirror—Use as standing, hanging, or hand mirror. One side is normal; the other side magnifies.
    G. Child's left-hand scissors—Four inches long.
    H. Adult's left-hand scissors—Made of finest steel.
    I. Kwik-Sip—Double walled drink dispenser, dishwasher proof. Comes apart easily for thorough cleaning. Unbreakable and spillproof. Keeps liquids cool for hours. Holds twelve ounces.
18. Monadnock Lifetime Products, Inc., Fitzwilliam, N.H. 03447
    A. Ice grippers for canes and crutches—Provides positive gripping and nonskid support on snow or ice. Grippers easily retracted for use indoors.
19. Nelson Medical Products, 5690 Sarah Avenue, Sarasota, Fla. 33583
    A. Adaptive eating utensils—Large slip-on swivel handle for utensils such as knives, forks, and spoons.
    B. Suction cup plates, scoop dishes for one-handed persons, as well as drinking straws made of plastic.
    C. Wide variety of dressing and grooming aids.
    D. Large supply of urinary catheters and supplies, and incontinent pants.
    E. Bed elevation blocks, mattress risers, blanket supports.
    F. Canes, crutches, walkers, orthopedic cushions, and so forth.
    G. Whistle switch—Plugs into TV, stereo, radio, lamp, or other appliances for remote control.
20. Ortho-Kinetics, Inc., P.O. Box 2000, Waukesha, Wis. 53187
    A. Cushion-Lift chair—Designed to help people who have difficulty getting to their feet. A touch of the control raises the seat slowly and safely.
    B. Cushion-Lift wheelchair.
    C. Activity chair with lift—Contact your nearest distributor or the factory for information or a home demonstration.
21. Piper Brace Sales Corporation, 811 Wyandotte Street, P.O. Box 807, Kansas City, Mo. 64141
    A. Padded arm sling—A quick, easy, and comfortable aid to immediate relief for a broken or sprained arm.
    B. Male and female Dri-pants.

C. Male easy-to-wear urinal.
D. Disposable heel and ankle protectors.

22. Ralco Manufacturing Company, 1537-A E. McFadden Avenue, Santa Ana, Calif. 92705
    A. EVER-SAFE—Effective safety garment for men, women, and children. Holds two sets of liners at one time for double capacity if needed. Protective Z pleats of the flannel liner overlay the "fluid barriers" so no plastic touches the skin, eliminating chafing. Not detectable under clothing. The entire garment may be conveniently slipped down over the hips without unfastening. Also have disposable throw-away liners.

23. Sheltered Workshop Inc., 200–204 Court Street, P.O. Box 310, Binghamton, N.Y. 19302
    A. Stocking device—To aid those who can't bend over to put on stockings or socks.

24. Spenco Medical Corporation, P.O. Box 8113, Waco, Tex. 76710
    A. Spenco cushion—Made from synthetic Gel—virtually identical in feel, weight, and pressure absorption to real tissue.
    B. Ostomy rings—Give freedom of body movement without leaking or embarrassment. Protects the skin.

25. Velcro, U.S.A., 681 5th Avenue, New York, N.Y. 10022
    A. Hook and loop fastener—Use instead of buttons, machine stitchable, goes on easy, holds tight. Best of all, it gives you a smooth professional look. Available by the inch, foot, or yard or in pre-cut Timesavers. Comes in six styles and ten colors. Available wherever notions are sold.

26. J.C. Wainright Distributors, 15099 Old Town, Riverview, Mich. 48192
    A. Have-a-Tray—You can carry things and still have both hands free to use your crutches, cane, walker, or wheelchair.

27. Winco Products, Winfield Company, Inc., 3062 46th Avenue North, St. Petersburg, Fla. 33714
    A. Safety rails and grab bars—Enables the infirm to help themselves; a safety feature that should be in every bath. Made of heavy anodized aluminum tubing. Flanges are stainless steel. Each rail is furnished with necessary fasteners to attach to any wall.
    B. Safety arm rest for toilets—Two models: Model #70—Front of seat rests on white plastic sleeves, will not mar seat or bowl; Model #90—floor model, does not change seat height. Front legs rest on tips, will not mar floor. Made for 16-inch high bowl. For lower bowl, shorten legs.
    C. Portable raised seat—For use where a permanent raised seat is not desired. Raises toilet seat 4 inches.

D. Shower seats—Two types: portable and folding seats. Portable unit has 3-inch suction cups that grip firmly. Folding unit attaches to any type wall.

Most of these suppliers have a wide variety of products other than those listed, and their catalogs are available free or for a small charge. Some products are listed several times to give you a choice in style, materials, and price.

chapter three
HOW'S YOUR FASHION IMAGE?

Everyone wants to be well dressed, and most of us like to keep up with current fashion trends. Today's new fashions can brighten your self-image and make you feel attractive. You can find clothing designed and manufactured with your special needs in mind whether you have difficulty managing buttons or zippers or have to cope with a wheelchair, brace, or crutches. And best of all, prices are becoming competitive with clothes for the nonhandicapped.

The following list includes a wide variety of sources for clothing for men, women, and children, plus a separate section on mastectomy clothes and products, alterations and sewing, tips for altering clothes, and other sewing hints. Included are suggestions for making a wheelchair, cane, or crutches a spirit-lifting part of your fashion image. There is also a word about clothing consultants and suggestions for choosing and caring for clothes.

Sources for Obtaining Clothes

1. Betty Butler, Inc., P.O. Box 51, Tenafly, N.J. 07670
    A. LapWrap—for the woman confined to a wheelchair. A unique design that looks like a full-length graceful skirt, but features a

cut-away back to avoid the problem of excess fabric bunching or getting wet. Full cut for comfortable fit and over-the-knee coverage with convenient Velcro fastener at waistband to provide adjustability and secure grip. Lightweight, with roomy easy-reach pockets with back opening for easy dressing while wearer is seated. Comes in several colors, average or large size.

B. Back-opening robes and dresses.

Double reversible zippers and an inside half belt make these jeans versatile and easy to wear over braces or prostheses. (Courtesy Clothing Research & Development, Milford, New Jersey.)

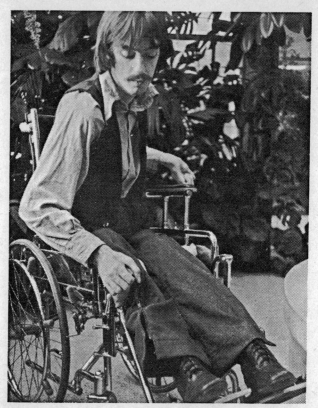

This view shows adaptations that can be used for wheelchair persons with extra allowance for shoes. (Courtesy Clothing Research & Development, Milford, New Jersey.)

2. CAPH Clothing, P.O. Box 22552, Sacramento, Calif. 95822—CAPH's Clothing for Handicapped Individual's Commission (LE CHIC) has published a manual in binder form. Included is information on reinforcing pants for braces, gusseting sleeves for extra reach, closures, dressing aids, adjusting patterns, and ready-to-wear clothing. It also has a bibliography, plus more. It sells for $6.00 and includes a periodic newsletter with more hints. New chapters may be purchased for $1.00 as they are written. Order from CAPH's LE CHIC at the address above.

3. Caradine of California, P.O. Box 22754, San Diego, Calif. 92122—Mrs. Carole Doolittle's company currently operates as a mail-order business. They sell ready-to-wear clothing in styles that include

This view shows how adaptable these can be for crutch users. (Courtesy Clothing Research & Development, Milford, New Jersey.)

women's pants, skirts, blouses, capes, nightgowns, and some children's clothes.
4. Care-Sew-Much Designs, 1920 Sheely Drive, Fort Collins, Colo. 80526
   A. Pantsuit—Two-piece with feet in and seat out.
   B. Bunting suit—Two-piece, skirt with seat out and cozy padded oval foot rest.
   C. Dress with yoke, set-in sleeves.
   D. Dress with raglan sleeves, gathered neck.
   E. Jumpsuits for men or women, men's night shirts, women's lace-trimmed nightgowns, plus several styles of wrap-around skirts.
5. Clothing Research and Development Foundation, Inc., P.O. Box 347, Milford, N.J. 08848—Functional fashions. For further information write to address above.

Front-closing bra. Three hooks in front make this very easy to slip into or out of. Tucks of nylon tricot provide perfect fit. (Courtesy FashionAble, Rocky Hill, New Jersey.)

6. Designs, Inc., P.O. Box 364, Stillwater, Okla. 74074—Write for further information.
7. FashionAble, Rocky Hill, N.J. 08553—Catalog costs 50¢.
   A. Bras
   Front-closing bra—Three hooks in front make this easy to slip into or out of.
   Front-snap bra—Single fastener. You can snap first and step in.
   Step-in bra—No fasteners at all. Even with only one hand, you can pull bra up over hips and shoulders.
   B. Slips
   Exclusive front-zippered slips—Simply step in and zip.
   Backwrap slip—Good for wheelchair use. Two Velcro closures in back. Machine washable.
   Bra-slip—Solve hip and bra problem with one garment. Plenty of stretch for step-in dressing. Nothing to fasten.
   Half slip for nearly everyone—Lies flat when opened. Held together with Velcro bands. Elastic waistband. Drip dry.
   C. Girdles
   Easy-on, easy-off girdles—Lightweight, no boning.
   Wrap-around garter belt—Satin covered Velcro bands hold belt around waist. Gives all support and control of conventional girdles.

Zip-front slip has a fourteen-inch zipper with small silk pull. Easy to shorten hem: just snip the stitches connecting the 1¼" band, leaving the remaining slip hemmed and ready to wear. (Courtesy FashionAble, Rocky Hill, New Jersey.)

Camisole. Good to wear under sheer tops or with slacks. Adjustable shoulder straps. Trimmed with soft lace. (Courtesy FashionAble, Rocky Hill, New Jersey.)

D. Dresses

Coat dress—Opens all the way. One row of nontarnish buttons. Washable. Choice of navy or off-white.

Frontwrap dress—Perky pretied bow conceals Velcro tab. Elasticized waist for comfort.

Wheelchair dress—Opens down back. Velcro tabs. Permanent press.

"Swirl" backwrap—This name has long been the best name in house dresses. Opens completely down the back. Generous overlap with wrap tie. One back button at top. Both tie and button can be converted to Velcro.

Gripper slipper is a comfortable and warm bed sock. Cozy terry slippers keep feet warm in bed or lounging. Bottom is slip resistant. (Courtesy FashionAble, Rocky Hill, New Jersey.)

    E. Pantsuits
       Pull-on pants with elastic band, no fasteners.
       Elastic waist slacks—No fasteners. Drip dry.
       Front-zip jumper—Basic, smart and simple. Wear with or without blouse.
    F. Vests—Most versatile, basic styles, close with Velcro tabs.

8. Geri Fashions, 301 E. Illinois, Newberg, Oreg. 97132
    A. Slips—Back opening, wide straps for comfort. White. Small, medium, large.
    B. Nightgowns—Below-the-knee length. Flannel or poly cotton pastel print. Small, medium, large.

9. Handee for You, 7674 Park Avenue, Lowville, N.Y. 13367—Offer service for women who wish to look attractive yet find it difficult to shop in a store, may be hard to fit or may have problems with dress closures. Offer a maximum of roomy comfort along with convenience, carefully engineered details, easy front closing, and a variety of necklines and sleeves and ample pockets.

    All clothes are semi-custom made. Order your regular size and they adapt each garment to suit individual needs. Directions for determining size and so forth included in catalog.
    Something new! Handee Kits—With the new Handee catalog this company offers a sew-it-yourself kit. If you can take advantage of the kits you will save approximately fifty percent of the cost of the ready-made garment. Catalog available for $1.00, which is refunded with first order.

Men and boys easy-on slacks. All-elastic waist. No buttons, zippers, or belts. Self-closing fly. One back pocket. Washable cotton-poly twill. (Courtesy FashionAble, Rocky Hill, New Jersey.)

The following items are available both ready made and in kits:

A. Tops and aprons—poncho, choice of fabric offered.
B. Tabard—resembles cobbler apron with divided pocket. Comes in short or long version.
C. Hoop apron—can be put on with one hand. Hoop removable for washing.
D. Robes—large sleeves, Velcro holds front closed, patch pocket.
E. Caftans—drop shoulder or cape sleeve caftan. Nylon jersey or polyester prints.
F. Sleep shirts—above knee length, patch pocket, close three fourths down with Velcro tabs. Open-back shirt—similar to above but opens in back.

10. I Can Do It Myself, 3773 Peppertree Drive, Eugene, Oreg. 97402
    A. Ladies shirt with square neck and raglan sleeves, long or short. Prints and solids. Sizes 28 through 44.
    B. Ladies skirt with three gores. Back panel omitted for comfort of

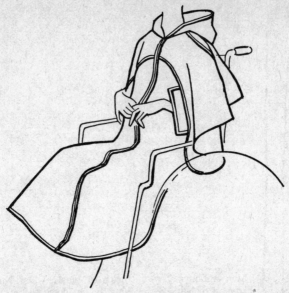

Wheelchair cape made of water-repellent poplin, resists wind and rain. Cut just below waist in back, covers knees and protects legs in front. Comfortable hood and seventeen-inch zipper. One size fits all. For men and women. (Courtesy FashionAble, Rocky Hill, New Jersey.)

those confined to a wheelchair. Elastic waist. Short or long length. Choice of colors. Sizes 30 to 40 (hip measurement).
C. Ladies blouse with front zipper—Choice of colors. Sizes: petite, small, medium, large, extra large.
D. Ladies dress with long front zipper—Can be worn loose or with self fabric belt. Choice of colors. Sizes: petite, small, medium, large, extra large.
E. Ladies cape, finger-tip length.
F. Men's dress shirt with easy-on features of raglan sleeves and Velcro closures on cuffs and down front. Long or short sleeves, plaid or solid colors. Sizes 34 through 44.
G. Men's shirt with collar, V-neck, raglan sleeves, long or short sleeves. Sizes 34 through 48.
H. Men's pants with pull-loops at waist and elastic waist back, Velcro fly closure. Options of Velcro side closure or pocket on lower pant leg. Sizes 28 through 38.

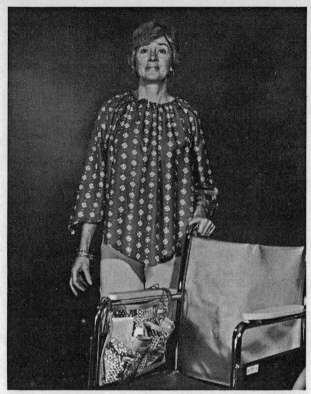

Handkerchief blouse. Over the head with adjustable neckline. Roomy raglan sleeves. Front, back, and sleeves fall into graceful positions. (Courtesy Handee For You, Lowville, New York.)

I. Men's jacket of quilted fabric. Spacious sleeves allow smooth dressing for those with limited arm movement. Velcro front closure, optional Velcro in back to open for easier dressing. Sizes 36 through 42.
J. Lower extremity wheelchair bag to keep your legs warm, comes to mid-thigh. Velcro strap for snug closure. Sizes for children and adults.
K. Wheelchair tote hooks on back of chair for carrying all your essentials.
L. Walker tote fits over walker with lots of pockets for carrying all your treasures.

Tabard. No side seams, adjustable waist tabs of Velcro. Divided pocket across bottom front. Shorter back for wheelchair persons, full length for ambulatory. (Courtesy Handee For You, Lowville, New York.)

    M. Knitted footwarmers, pull-on style that stays on securely and keeps your feet cozy. Comes in small, medium, or large.

For children, there are boys' and girls' shirts and pants in several styles, girls' dresses, tops, jumpers, and much more.

11. Iowa State University, Cooperative Extension Service, Ames, Iowa 50011—A booklet entitled CLOTHES TO FIT YOUR NEEDS is available from the Publications Distribution Department. The booklet covers information about clothing, such as attractiveness, comfort, safety, convenience, and care. It covers choosing new clothes as well as altering those you already have to meet your individual need, whether you use a wheelchair, crutches, or whatever. The booklet is available at a minimal charge.

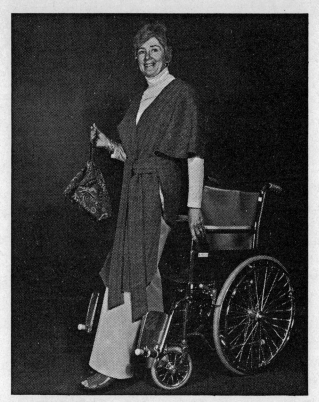

Stole with shaped shoulders, no side seams or front closures. Short in back for sitters, full length for ambulatory. (Courtesy Handee For You, Lowville, New York.)

12. Jacksonville State University, Jacksonville, Ala. 36265—A pamphlet is available that tells you how to fashion your own undergarments from standard ones available on the market or how you can make them at home. Covers directions for altering or making half slips, full slips, "seat-less" slips, all types of bras, and so forth. The booklet is entitled UNDERGARMENTS FOR THOSE WITH SPECIAL NEEDS.

13. Lawson Hill Leather and Shoe Company, 580 Winter Street, Waltham, Mass. 02254—(Toll-free telephone number—800-343-8500)—A catalog is available that lists hard-to-find sizes of shoes for both men and women. Offers a wide variety of styles and sizes. Order sheet included.

14. Piper Brace Company, 811 Wyandotte Street, Kansas City, Mo. 64141

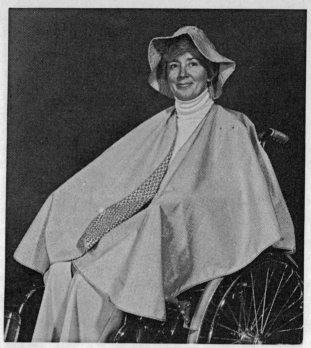

Rain cape. Slips over shoulders like a poncho. No closures. Waterproof fabric. (Courtesy Handee For You, Lowville, New York.)

  A. Female Dri pants—Here is peace of mind for the millions of women who suffer from urinary incontinency or need a special garment to wear after surgery. Snap-in pads are lined with a special "keep dry" fabric that allows only a one-way moisture flow—away from the body. Skin stays drier, more comfortable. Completely washable, smooth fitting, invisible under clothing. Order by waist measurement.

  B. Male Dri support—Easy, sanitary way to stop the embarrassment of wet garments and bedding. Day and night support that gives you constant protection and confidence. Elastic belt, wetproof pouch. Reusable cotton pad snaps in, removes easily for laundering. Order by waist measurement.

15. Self-Help Clothing for Handicapped Children, Easter Seal Society, 2023 West Ogden Avenue, Chicago, Ill. 60612—The Society publishes a guide that brings together practical adaptions, and proven ideas and suggestions for clothing that children can manage them-

selves. It discusses and illustrates outer apparel and undergarments that are both functional and attractive and presents designs evolved from the experience of parents and therapists. It gives guidelines for selection or simple alteration of all articles in a child's wardrobe, so that he or she may be independent in this aspect of daily living no matter what the handicap or the individual need.

16. Sheltered Workshop for the Disabled, 200 Court Street, P.O. Box 310, Binghamton, N.Y. 13902
    A. Stocking pull-on device for both men and women. Complete instructions for use are enclosed with each device sold.

17. Special Publications, Accent on Living, Box 700, Bloomington, Ill. 61701—They offer a booklet entitled CLOTHING DESIGNS FOR THE HANDICAPPED, which covers designing clothes for persons with limited finger, arm, and hand movement; those using crutches or wearing braces or casts; women who have had mastectomies; persons using wheelchairs; the elderly; the overweight; the incontinent; and the blind. Geared to the average home sewer, this booklet will prove valuable to professionals, the disabled, and their families.

Wraparound jumper. (Courtesy Textile Research Center, Texas Tech University, Lubbock, Texas.)

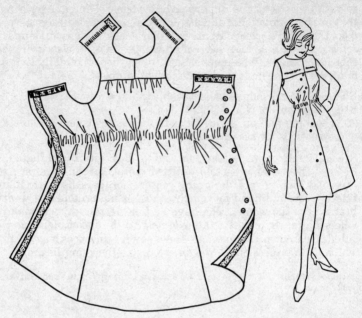

Wraparound dress. (Courtesy Textile Research Center, Texas Tech University, Lubbock, Texas.)

18. Texas Tech University, Box 5217, Lubbock, Tex. 79417—Designs by Kay Caddel, research associate, are produced through the Textile Research Center, Texas Tech University, in cooperation with the Natural Fibers and Food Protein Commission of Texas. They also offer a pamphlet entitled PATTERN DESIGNS FOR THE PHYSICALLY AND MENTALLY HANDICAPPED.
- A. Smock—loose fitting from yoke down, has front opening and large armholes.
- B. Jumper—side openings with separating zipper, front opening at waistline. Easy access through neck opening.
- C. Dress—dress lies flat, front and yoke openings, elastic waistline. For ease in dressing nonambulatory persons.
- D. Jacket—two front separating zippers, back pleats for extra room, lapels without collar.
- E. Jeans—outside pockets, front fly, elastic back waistband with entire front openings on each leg.
- F. Wrap-around skirt and blouse—skirt wraps in back, ties in front. Peasant blouse, fullness contained with elastic in neck and sleeves.

Wraparound skirt and blouse. (Courtesy Textile Research Center, Texas Tech University, Lubbock, Texas.)

    G. Jumpsuit—either front or back zipper. Side opening optional.
    H. Wrap slacks—front portion hooks together in back with an elastic strap. Back can be lowered and raised separately. For persons in a wheelchair.
    I. Gown—hospital-type gown with extra section to cover hip area.
    J. Wheelchair items—Vest, wheelchair support, utility lap tray, tote bag, box-lap bag.
19. TechniFlair, Box 40, Cotter, Ariz. 72626
    A. Pants—elastic back or all elastic waistband in shorts or pull-on slacks. Wide variety of solid colors and patterns. Sizes: small, medium, large.
    B. Pull-over tops with round or V-neck, in wide variety of colors. Sizes: small, medium, large.
    C. Dresses—front or back opening, wide variety of colors and sizes.
    D. Wheelchair dress—Self fabric ties fasten behind chair back for support. Fastens with Velcro at waist and shoulder. Variety of colors and patterns.
    E. Back-wrap chair robes—short sleeves, wide scoop neck. Velcro

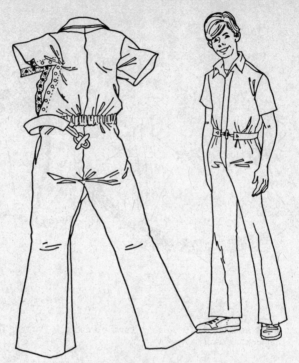

Jumpsuit. (Courtesy Textile Research Center, Texas Tech University, Lubbock, Texas.)

closures at neck and waist. Long self ties at under arm seams and front waist.
F. Front-fastening slip with side straps. Back-opening slip has gripper snap closures.
G. Bed gowns—front opening with gripper snap closures. Back opening with generous overlap for modesty.
H. Men's pants—all elastic waistband or elastic back band.
I. Slacks for nonambulatory male. Zipper sewn in crotch cross seam. Extra length in back keeps pants from riding up. Assorted solid colors and plaids. Sizes: small, medium, large.
J. Special pants for physically handicapped, both sides open with Velcro closure for individuals with orthopedic disabilities or wearing prosthetic devices—for the nonambulatory or incontinent.

Hospital-type gown with extra section to cover hip areas. (Courtesy Textile Research Center, Texas Tech University, Lubbock, Texas.)

K. Side-opening shirts for both men and women with orthopedic disabilities. Long-sleeved shirt opens full length of side seam.
L. Adult bibs.

20. University of Alabama, Office of Independent Study, P.O. Box 2967, University, Ala. 35486—Offers a booklet entitled ADAPT YOUR OWN, which covers ideas for clothing adaptation for individuals who are wheelchair-bound or limb deficient, those who have limited mobility of hands or arms, limited or weak finger action, poor coordination, or limited vision, those who use crutches, or those who are incontinent. The booklet is available for $2.00.

21. Vocational Guidance and Rehabilitation Services, 2239 East 55th Street, Cleveland, Ohio 44103—Catalog available for $1.00.
    A. Sleepwear—front- and back-opening gowns and nightshirts. Robes with front or back openings.
    B. Slips and half slips in a variety of styles.
    C. Dresses—backwrap dresses that come with a choice of eight or ten different necklines plus several other dress styles.
    D. Skirts, jumpers, blouses—a variety of styles.
    E. Slacks for both men and women—open front or back and any combination of leg seam opening needed.
    F. Stocking pull-on.

Basic backwrap dress. Four back fasteners (Velcro or grippers), generous back overlap. Two waist adjustments and elastic at waist for comfortable expansion. Two generous pockets on shirt. (Courtesy Vocational Guidance and Rehabilitation Services, Cleveland, Ohio.)

For children, they have the following items.
G. Sleepwear for children—front- or back-opening gowns and nightshirts. All sizes.
H. Dresses—one style with three different bibs.
I. Boys slacks and shirts in different styles and sizes.
J. Underclothing for all sizes.

Mastectomy Clothes and Products

1. Airway Surgical Company, Erie Avenue, Cincinnati, Ohio 45209
   A. Silicone external breast prosthesis—looks natural, feels natural, and moves naturally. Designed to be worn in any well-fitting bra.
   B. Silk and Qiana bras in a variety of styles with matching half slips. Light, flexible underwire delicately shapes cups and provides excellent separation and support of both the natural

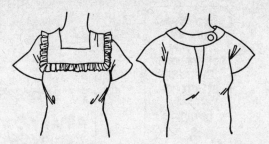

Some neck variations for backwrap dress. (Courtesy Vocational Guidance and Rehabilitation Services, Cleveland, Ohio.)

and artificial breast. A three-quarter-length style designed for the fuller figure with either front or back closure.

These bras are available in many department stores such as Bullocks, Liberty House, Emporium-Capwell, as well as in many lingerie shops. If unable to locate these bras in your area, Airway will mail you a list of the stores that carry their products.

2. Reflections, 230 Park Avenue, New York, N.Y. 10169—Catalog available.
   A. LiteMate forms to wear with nightgowns and leisure daytime fashions.
   B. Bra with a wide band under the bust for extra support, and comfortably wide built-up shoulder straps adjust in back for a smooth look.
   C. Full slip with wide camisole straps and modesty cut neckline.
   D. Swimsuit—tank-type suit with moderately cut neckline and comfortable cap sleeves for added coverage.
   E. Two-piece plunge suit with bottom that adjusts with drawstrings from a full panty to a bikini. Top has scoop back.
   F. Skirted suit with additional tummy control in front panel, available with jacket and matching short or long skirt.

3. Regenesis, Inc., 18 East 53rd Street, New York, N.Y. 10022—This is a New York boutique that specializes exclusively in fitting women who have had mastectomies. "Because we treat each fitting individually, we have developed many creative solutions to the various fitting problems. Our expert fitters have designed new methods of achieving a smooth and even look for everyone, even if there is a hollow that can't be corrected by a prosthesis alone." Also accepts orders by mail; catalog available.
   A. Swimsuits
      Completely adjustable, two-piece, full panty adjusts to bikini.

After breast surgery... Airway Companion II. A good reason for confidence.

Nothing could be more natural. And no one will ever know the difference.
 The Airway Companion II looks and feels like you. It's 100% silicone. It's wash and wear. And there's no need for a special bra.
 You can wear the Airway Companion II with your regular lingerie, and you can wear it when you play your favorite sports. It will fit bra sizes 32A through 44D. And Airway has a full line of beautiful swimwear for you.
 Beauty, comfort, and confidence. Airway Companion II is the finest natural breast replacement you can buy.
 Covered by Medicare and many other major medical plans.

Airway Companion II

After breast surgery... Airway Companion II. Beautiful, stylish, and totally feminine.

Elegant brassieres with a lacey look. And the choice of styles!
 The delicate, youthful Bandeau. A light, flexible underwire bandeau shapes the bosom and gives excellent separation and support of both the natural and artificial breast.
 The flattering Princess ¾ length molds and minimizes the fuller breast, creating a natural contour. And Airway's uniquely designed Companion Leisure Bra combines the princess cut with a matchmate lining, creating a pleasing line for the sheerest outerwear.
 Featuring a bobbinet power lace elastic waist band, Airway's lovely Princess Long Line supports and slims. And all of Airway's high-fashion brassieres are designed to conform with every movement of your figure.
 Totally feminine, totally you!

Airway Companion II

After breast surgery... Airway Companion II® Enjoy life the way you always have.

Enjoy yourself! Beauty and confidence are designed into this stylish collection of Airway swimwear created especially for you.
 Swim, sunbathe and play like you always have in attractively cut maillots and skirts with day and evening wear cover-ups.
 Unique convertible necklines can be closed — or opened to show a flattering V-line. And all styles have a soft-cup construction with a set-in brassiere and inner pockets.
 With an array of beautiful patterns, our Airway swimwear line will enhance your appearance from any viewpoint.
 Sophisticated swimwear for you. Another fashion idea from Airway.

Airway Companion II

(Courtesy Airway Surgical Company, Cleveland, Ohio.)

Short sleeved mioleg suit. Neckline at the collarbone, scooped neck. (Courtesy Regenesis, Inc.)

Short-sleeved skirted suit.

One-piece suit with empire waist, button front, and keyhole back.

Short-sleeved, one-piece suit.

B. Nightgowns

All nightgowns have exclusive Sleep Puff, a lightweight and comfortable prosthesis that can be worn in nightgowns and lounge wear.

Long gown with scooped neckline trimmed with lace and self beading trim lace around armholes and down sides.

Completely adjustable two-piece. Tighten the ribbon through the center seam for the exact neckline you want. Fully panty, adjusts to bikini (Courtesy Regenesis, Inc.)

OTHER SOURCES OF
MASTECTOMY BRAS
AND BREAST FORMS

Many department stores, lingerie shops, and surgical specialty houses carry prosthetic devices, bras, and special clothing. You may want to look at several because there are many different types and materials; also, prices vary considerably from one place to another.

Alterations and Sewing

1. Bernina Sewing Machines, Bernina Distributors Inc., 2401 South Hill Street, Los Angeles, Calif. 90007—The Bernina Handicap model sewing machine is basically the same design as their standard model, with its acclaimed advantages of simple operation, reliability, and high performance. The Handicap model is supplied with all essential accessories plus additional features, such as a presser-foot that can be changed without screws, a finger guard to prevent in-

Grecian fitted gown lavished with appliqued lace. (Courtesy Regenesis, Inc.)

juries from the needle, an adjustable stop to guide the work, a presser-foot lever to raise and lower the presser-foot, a speed regulator operated by elbow or knee (a neck belt is also available for operation with the chin), a special holder for removal and insertion of bobbin case, a machine needle with slot to the eye, and a lever for turning the handwheel.

If you can't find the machine for sale locally, write to the company, and they will tell you where the nearest distributor is located.

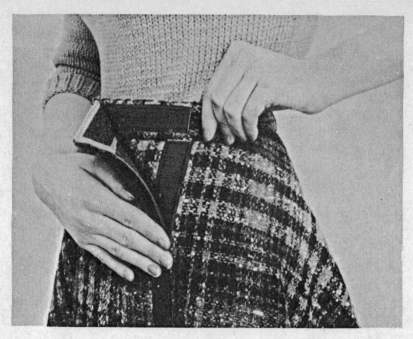

Velcro self-adhesive fasteners can solve the problem when buttons or zippers are too difficult to manage. (Courtesy VELCRO USA, Inc., New York, New York.)

2. VELCRO, USA, 681 5th Avenue, New York, N.Y. 10022—Brochures or pamphlets can be obtained by writing to the company. Velcro products are also available from notion or sewing sections of most department or fabric stores. Velcro has the following uses:
   A. Can replace hooks and eyes or snaps on waistbands.
   B. For closing blouses, skirts, shirts, and pants. Can be secured with a gentle touch and opened with a slight pull. Eliminates use of buttons, hooks, and other hard-to-manage closures.
   C. Coin-sized pieces of Velcro can be sewn under the front edges of blouses or shirts. The buttons can be sewn on top and the look is the same.
   D. Velcro works well for seam closures. If you have a broken arm or leg, seams can be opened and equipped with Velcro closings, which can later be removed and the seams resewn.

Velcro self-adhesive fasteners provide smooth, easy closures. (Courtesy VELCRO USA, Inc., New York, New York.)

Available as follows:

A. Comes in inch, foot, or yard lengths and in various widths.
B. Ten-inch, all-purpose strips.
C. Circles and squares.
D. Handy pre-cut, pre-basted shapes in six styles and ten colors.
E. Circles and squares in three convenient sizes replace buttonholes and snaps. Choice of light, medium, or heavy stress.

The Velcro self-adhesive tape gives this slip a smooth, tailored fit without the need to pull it on over the head or struggle into it feet first. (Courtesy VELCRO USA, Inc., New York, New York.)

Tips for Altering Clothes

1. A bathrobe or dressing gown using one-inch squares of Velcro stitched in place of buttons is easier to manage than long strips of Velcro.

2. If braces or crutches cause extra wear in certain areas, you can make a patch to fit inside the garment or perhaps put a decorative one on the outside. Those worn next to the skin should be made of soft, smooth, absorbent material, such as cotton flannel,

cotton and rayon, or polyester blends. Reinforce inside of slacks for braces by adding an extra layer of fabric.

3. If blouse or shirt comes out of slacks or skirt, you can add extra fabric to lengthen the garment, finish edges and wear outside, or remake it into a body shirt. (One man said that his shirt tail often failed to "cover the subject" when he was in the wheelchair. He solved the problem by having his shirts that are worn on the outside slit up the sides and hemmed so they wouldn't slide up.)

4. If long sleeves pull up and are uncomfortable when using your crutches, you can cut and make short sleeves or make a gusset under the arm for extra room when shortening the sleeves is impractical.

5. The mother of a teenage boy who broke his leg and who was very depressed at the prospect of having his trousers pinned up for the duration of his cast, solved the problem for him. She slit the inner seam of his pants and sewed several twenty-two-inch zippers in the seam. This enabled him to dress and undress with ease. When the cast was removed, so were the zippers, and the seam was sewn back up. Good as new!

6. Elastic can eliminate the necktie problem. Tie the knot, cut a piece from the portion that goes under the collar and replace it with enough elastic so the tie will slip over the head.

7. Elastic is great for adapting belts, buttons, and waistbands. Belts can be buckled, then cut apart and the elastic sewn under the buckle overlap where it won't show at all, or in back where it is hidden by the wheelchair.

8. The loafer or pump-type shoe is the simplest to wear unless you have to consider transferring to or from a wheelchair. However, elastic shoe laces are now available and they make wearing other types of shoes possible.

9. Many fabric handbags or tote bags can be adapted for easy closing and protection of contents by adding strips of Velcro.

Sewing Hints

1. Electric scissors make the task of cutting much easier. They are available at department, sewing machine, or fabric stores.

2. Left-hand scissors are available from most department stores.

3. You can use a magnet to pick up pins when grasp or vision is limited.

4. Automatic needle threaders are available from FashionAble and other mail-order stores. They are also available from department, fabric, and sewing stores.

5. One wheelchair seamstress recommends plastic-headed silk pins because they are easy to handle. She keeps them in a magnetized container so she doesn't drop them.

6. Because commercial patterns need so many adjustments, she works from basic patterns cut from a special nylon fabric. It is as easy to pin and see through as tissue paper but does not tear or wrinkle. They are available from Trace and Fit, P.T.I., Box 511, Old Chelsea Station, New York, N.Y. 10011.

Brighten Your Wheelchair, Cane, or Crutches

Wheelchairs, canes, and crutches don't have to be drab and ugly. One woman had her husband spray her wooden cane a bright pink to match a new outfit. She was so pleased with the result that she had him spray several more in different colors. She keeps them hanging in the hall closet and chooses one to match her outfit whenever she goes out.

One man tapes an artificial flower to the front of his cane, just clear of the crook to leave space enough for his hand. He has a collection of plastic flowers of different colors and varieties to suit the season, his outfit, or holiday, such as poinsettias at Christmas or daffodils in the spring. He finds most of them at thrift shops or rummage sales so his cheerful spot of color costs practically nothing.

An entertainer who was on crutches thought the plain old crutch looked awful when she wore her long evening gowns on stage so she had fabric covers made to match her dresses.

Wheelchairs can be dressed up to match the user's clothes, mood, age, hobby, or whatever else is desired. One woman fashions wheelchair outfits the way other women sew dresses. She

cuts enough fabric to cover the entire backrest and seat of the
chair, allowing extra length for hemming. The material can be
fastened to the chair with buttons, hooks, snaps, or loops, depending on the design of the chair. Side panels can be made of fabric,
contact wallpaper, or applique placed on cardboard which, in
turn, is fastened to the metal side of the wheelchair with rubber
bands or masking tape.

Others cover the entire backrest in various materials featuring designs on cloth, canvas, paper, or cardboard. These can be
fastened with Velcro tabs, snaps, or loops so that they can be
changed as desired. One teenager has a mounted poster of a
motorcycle and the caption "Easy Rider" on his chair. Fabric de-
picting animals, Raggedy Ann and Andy, or other storybook
characters can be used for a child's wheelchair cover.

Manufacturers are beginning to recognize the need for more
color and design instead of the drab colors that were for too long
the only ones available. Wheelchairs now come in prints with
trims in solid colors. Canes are appearing on the market made of
plastic with colorful flowers and other objects imbedded in the
mold.

One veterans hospital reports that every wheelchair fitted
there is upholstered in colors selected by the patient.

Clothing Consultants

Eleanor Greenshields, Personal Wardrobe Consultant, P.O. Box
31014, San Francisco, Calif. 94131—A personal wardrobe consultant will save you time, money, and frustrating shopping
experiences, and you will look and feel your best. They can offer
personal wardrobe consultation, usually in the customers' home,
to help them plan a wardrobe around their individual clothing
needs—one that will work best for them. You may be able to find
one listed in your telephone directory.

Choice of Clothing

1. Well-constructed clothing wears longer and cuts down on
troublesome repairs. Seams that are finished and reinforced for
strength help prevent damage to clothing.

2. Choose fabrics that have good wearing qualities, don't wrinkle easily, are comfortable and attractive to wear, and are easy to clean and care for.

3. Make a list of your special requirements before you shop for clothes. This eliminates getting carried away with something you like in the store and then when you get home finding it too much of a hassle to put on or take off.

4. Maternity shops often carry clothes that the woman in a wheelchair or one with limited arm motion can use. Stretchable front panels in slacks and skirts make them easier to get into, and many maternity tops and dresses have front openings.

5. Short jackets are more comfortable than long ones for wheelchair use. Sitting on bunched-up fabric is uncomfortable.

6. For extra warmth, take your cue from the athlete. Select leg warmers, leotards such as ballet dancers wear, thermal underwear, down-filled vests or bootees, such as skiers, hunters, and other outdoor sports people use.

7. For the woman with the use of only one arm, a poncho is more convenient and stays on better than a shawl or stole. It also is a good cover-up for an amputee or the person with a useless arm or other deformity.

8. For the man in a wheelchair, mid-length boxer-type shorts stay in place better than the shorter jockey styles. They are not so apt to bind. Shorts without seams are more comfortable when sitting for long periods. Boxer shorts slip on more easily when reach is limited or when wearing braces because there is more room in the leg area. Knit briefs tend to get caught on the locks of braces.

9. A T-shirt should always be worn under braces or insets to protect the skin from rubbing and to absorb perspiration.

10. Avoid wearing slippers of knit, synthetic, terrycloth, or other soft fabrics unless slippers have hard soles that can be roughened to prevent slipping and falling.

11. For the one-hander, choosing clothing with pockets is extremely important, both for convenience and comfort. You can carry small items in them or you can place an unusable hand inside for warmth or to hold it steady.

12. Pantsuits take the attention away from the legs. Wider pant legs conceal leg bags.

13. A long skirt is graceful and concealing both for wheelchair and leg braces.

14. Boxy jackets, cardigans, and loose-fitting blouses worn over skirts or pants can hide back braces.

15. To avoid the problem of blouse or shirt coming out of skirt or slacks, choose shirts with long tails or body shirts. Or choose tops to wear outside of skirt or slacks.

16. Select front-opening garments or those that slip easily over your head.

17. Tube socks have no heel or toe and are easier to put on for anyone with reaching or bending problems or for those with limited vision.

18. When possible, select garments that are appropriate for all seasons. For example, a waterproof all-weather coat with detachable lining is useful all year round.

19. Plan your clothing needs around one or two basic colors.

20. Coordinated separates you can mix or match are good wardrobe extenders.

21. For wheelchair wear keep sleeves elbow length or shorter. Long sleeves tend to wear out too fast by rubbing against the wheel.

22. Pullovers or loose cowl necks are easy to get on and much neater looking than cardigans, which tend to bunch when sitting. They also tend to gap between buttons.

Caring for Your Clothes—Handy Hints

1. You can keep leather or patent leather shoes cleaned and polished by using a spray-on polish that requires no rubbing or buffing. Also, Esquire's Quick-Ease throw-away shoeshine pads are available in several colors. They can be purchased at shoe stores, department stores, or drug and variety stores.

2. There are some aerosol spot removers that dry to powder and leave no ring. They are available in many department stores.

3. Many outer garments can be sprayed with Scotch Guard or a similar substance that repels spots and stains. Many spills can just be wiped off with a damp cloth, cutting down on cleaning bills.

4. Large plastic bibs can keep food stains and spots off clothing.

5. A plastic apron can keep clothes clean when putting on make-up, doing household chores, and many other activities while either standing up or sitting in a wheelchair.

6. Using padded hangers keep garments from losing their shape and needing frequent pressing.

7. A small bathroom plunger can be used by the person with one hand to plunge clothes up and down through sudsy water instead of trying to rub or scrape by hand.

8. A small clothesline and pins found in travel kits are just great for hanging small items in your own bathroom.

chapter four
SHORTCUTS TO HOUSEWORK

Housework is a chore for most of us and we are always looking for ways to do things quicker, easier, and more efficiently. Whether you have an arm or leg in a cast or a permanent disability, you may need to find new ways of doing things in order to get the job done at all.

The following suggestions come from people who have limited motion in some parts of their bodies but who are coping with many household tasks. The following examples will give you a number of choices or will perhaps trigger ideas you can adapt to your own limitations.

Organizing Your Work

Make your work schedule a flexible one so you don't try to do too much on any one day. Set priorities, realizing that nearly every chore can be completed in segments. Break up heavy work like ironing or cleaning over several days. If you can't manage everything, straighten and dust the living room and tidy up the kitchen, as these are the two rooms you spend the most time in. Everything will look nice if people drop in and you can do the bedrooms later.

If you tend to tire easily some days and have more energy on others, as is the case if you have multiple sclerosis or arthritis, it helps to alternate the heavier tasks with less strenuous ones. You might want to vacuum one room and then fold some clothes or read for awhile, then vacuum the second room and so on. If you feel really tired, lie down periodically.

Ask yourself: Does it have to be done by me or can someone else do it? Can someone else in the family do it or can I hire someone to do it? Can I send the laundry out? Can I send the baby to a nursery school? Is there an easier way to do it?

Find the most comfortable position to do a job and use that position. Slide things, don't lift them. Use a rolling table to move things.

See that all family members have tasks assigned to them according to age and ability. Even three- and four-year-olds can empty waste baskets, fetch and carry for you, carry their own dishes to the sink, put knives and forks on the table. As they get older they can make their own beds, take care of their own rooms, help with the laundry, help with the cooking, vacuum, and do the inevitable dishes.

Teenagers should be able to do any and all housekeeping tasks, cook a meal, do the shopping, and care for their own clothes including washing and ironing.

If no family members are available, consider having a high school girl come in one or two afternoons a week or on Saturday to do the things you can't manage, or have a janitorial service come in periodically to do the heavy chores.

Substitutes for Cleaning Tools Too Heavy or Awkward to Use

FROM THE TOY COUNTER

1. A toy broom does a great job of sweeping up spilled soap powder or cornflakes, of reaching hard-to-get-at corners around the furniture, and of keeping the sand from the cat's litter box brushed into the corner until it can be vacuumed. The broom can be wrapped with a dust cloth to reach those cobwebs on closet ceilings, walls, or in corners.

2. A child's dustmop reaches under beds and dressers and does a quick dusting of a whole floor or the borders around area rugs.

3. Toy carpet sweepers often work well for a quick pickup of crumbs on rugs and floors between more thorough jobs of vacuuming.

FROM THE SUPERMARKET

1. Most supermarkets carry small dish mops that can perform many other useful chores. I keep one in each bathroom to clean the walls when they get spattered, especially around the washbowl and under the towel racks. They are also handy to mop up steamy drips from shower and tub or to clean the woodwork around the door knobs or even the whole door. The mop is easier to use than a sponge that has to be squeezed frequently.

2. A small vegetable brush is great for scrubbing ash trays, sink faucets and fixtures, cookie tins, or any other small scrubbing jobs that are hard for sore, stiff fingers to manage.

3. A pair of vegetable tongs is a versatile tool to have on hand. Try using them for turning pieces of meat in the roaster or under the broiler, lifting hard-boiled eggs out of the water, or grasping pickles from a jar. You can also use them to pick up small objects dropped on the floor or to get small cans or boxes out of reach on the cupboard shelf.

FROM THE DEPARTMENT STORE

1. The ironing board has unlimited possibilities because of its adjustable height and because it can be easily carried from one room to another. Putting your portable sewing machine on it enables you to sew or mend at a comfortable height. Covered with a sheet of plastic or oilcloth, it provides a good work surface for any sitdown cleaning job from polishing the silverware to peeling vegetables or folding the laundry.

2. A yardstick can be used for many reaching jobs—it can close furnace vents and adjust the tops of your drapes. Slip one or two old socks over the end and secure them with a rubber band for a handy duster or for cleaning under the refrigerator, stove, or other furniture too low for the vacuum cleaner.

3. A square of nylon net makes a fabulous scrub cloth; you can stitch it into a ball and keep one in the kitchen and one in the bathroom. The net is scratchy enough to clean, yet it won't hurt your fingers. It can clean anything from the bathtub to the kitchen stove without damaging any of your painted surfaces. You can also use it to scrub potatoes for baking and to clean fresh mushrooms. The nylon is easy to handle, easy to wash, and requires no wringing and squeezing.

Housekeeping Hints

1. Spray and wipe-off cleaners are ideal for the disabled housekeeper. Using them eliminates carrying a mixture that may slosh on the floor as you carry it. The bottle and a sponge can be easily carried and eliminates the rinsing necessary with any other products. Wiping fingerprints off of walls, woodwork, and appliances is no longer a major task.

2. It may be easier to dust all the furniture in the house in one day rather than do each room separately. You save energy by getting out and putting away the dust cloths, furniture polish, or whatever else you need only once instead of several times. If you have difficulty holding the dust cloth, try using old cotton socks. Put them on your hands.

3. Vacuuming can be easier with a lightweight electric broom; some people prefer a cleaner that moves about on wheels with hose and wands light enough to handle easily. A small, lightweight hand vacuum can be used for the furniture and other small cleaning jobs.

4. Cleaning the bathtub can be done with a short-handled dish mop or Johnny Mop with a disposable head. There are many bath preparations that leave no rings on the tub and so reduce cleaning to a minimum.

5. A toy broom and a long-handled dustpan are useful for sweeping small areas.

6. See which works best for you—a regular broom, pushbroom, or dust mop. They are available from Stanley Home Products parties, Fuller Brush, or wherever housewares are sold. If the handles are too long for you, they can be cut to any convenient length.

7. A sponge mop is usually easier to handle and there are some that can be wrung out with little exertion.

8. Line your shelves with plastic or other washable material so you can wipe them off rather than change them.

9. Put castors on your heavy pieces of furniture so you don't have to pull and tug when cleaning.

10. Spray-on cleaners work well for washbasins. Toilet bowls can be done without too much trouble and the bases can be reached with a short mop.

11. Use paper products whenever possible
    A.   Paper napkins eliminate the need for cloth ones that require laundering.
    B.   A paper cup dispenser in your bathroom and kitchen cuts down on washing glasses, is safer to use, and keeps colds from spreading from one family member to another.
    C.   A roll of paper towels in the bathroom and kitchen is great for drying hands, wiping up spills, cleaning out the cat's litter box, and for cleaning mirrors, etc.
    D.   Keep paper guest towels in the bathroom for company.
    E.   Use placemats that can be wiped with a damp sponge rather than mats or tablecloths that have to be laundered. Some very lovely plastic tablecloths are available that need a minimum of care.

12. Put up a bulletin board in the kitchen and other suitable areas for notices, clippings, lists, etc. You can see them at a glance and change them with little effort.

13. Learn to "top clean" so your house or apartment will have the appearance of being neat and uncluttered. Take a large paper sack as you go to empty ash trays, discard newspapers, and gather miscellaneous junk.

14. Places for a cane user to stand the cane when working in the kitchen can be fashioned from all-leather loops or strips of Velcro fastened to the counter edge at intervals around the kitchen.

15. Spray cans offer the easiest method of handling many household tasks for a homemaker who has the use of only one hand or who must conserve strength in hands or wrists. Use spray cans to do the following:
    A.   Polish the furniture.
    B.   Clean your shoes.

    C. Starch the clothes.
    D. Clean mirrors and bathroom fixtures.
    E. Preserve furnishings and clothing.

16. Shelf paper won't tear as easily and it is less effort to secure it with Scotch tape rather than thumbtacks.

17. A flip-top plastic wastebasket stored in each bedroom closet makes a convenient clothes hamper.

18. Use cold-water detergent to clean plastic fashion accessories, such as handbags, belts, and shoes. Just apply detergent to a damp sponge, clean the accessory, then rinse with another sponge dampened in cold water.

19. A toothbrush is a versatile tool for all sorts of small jobs. It's good for:
    A. Cleaning deeply engraved silver pieces and tableware, as well as polishing brass andirons, trivets, and so forth.
    B. Cleaning marble-topped tables.
    C. Restoring grout to its original color and cleaning ceramic tiles in bathroom or kitchen.
    D. Cleaning the burners on your gas range.
    E. Bringing a sparkle to your diamond rings and other jewelry.
    F. Cleaning out the crumbs from inside the toaster. (Be sure it's unplugged before you start the job.)

20. Coat your dustpan with a layer of wax—you'll find it won't retain dust and dirt particles and trash will slide off easily.

21. To clean woodwork quickly and easily, make a solution of equal parts of vinegar, water, and kerosene. Apply with a soft cloth.

22. To clean ivory piano keys and keep them from turning yellow, rub them with a soft cloth dampened with warm sweet milk.

23. Those small cotton-tipped swabs are great for cleaning grooves in sliding doors, around the dials and knobs of radio and TV sets, appliances, carved furniture, small objects on the whatnot shelf, and so forth. Dampen with cold water or detergent suds when needed. The same swabs are great for applying paste or glue.

24. Clean your telephone with a cleaner-polisher wax. This leaves a protective coat that prevents soiling.

25. Glass or ceramic lamp bases clean easily when they are

wiped with one of the spray-on liquid glass cleaners. Polish the bases dry.

26. Fumbling for a light switch or keyhole in the dark is frustrating. Using luminous paint or tape (which comes in rolls) to mark them is helpful. Also good to mark edges of basement or garage steps and many other places or items.

27. Wallpaper is wider and thicker than regular shelf paper, and it comes in different widths, which makes it wonderful for lining those deep linen closet shelves and dresser drawers. If you buy broken rolls or ends, you can get some good bargains. It is also good for making place mats; cut with pinking shears to make attractive edges.

28. An automatic timer can be put to many uses, such as monitoring phone calls, limiting tasks so you don't become too tired (iron for half an hour and stop when the timer goes off), timing the lawn sprinklers or garden hoses, or as a reminder when the dryer will stop so you can remove clothes that wrinkle if not taken out immediately.

29. The small plastic containers in which berries, cherry tomatoes, or sprouts are sold are great to put on your medicine shelf to hold small bottles that tip over easily or tubes of ointment, and so forth. They can also be used in a sewing drawer to hold spools of thread, cards of snaps, and other small items. In a dresser drawer they can hold any number of small objects including the tags that come with new clothes giving the washing and cleaning instructions.

30. Instead of keeping soap dishes on your bathroom and kitchen sink, use colored sponges. They keep the soap from melting and you don't have a messy soapdish to clean. Another advantage is always having a soapy sponge handy for quick cleaning jobs.

31. Telephone tips—An extension phone in the bedroom or den can save a lot of steps. And a phone with a long cord can be carried wherever you need it. Or you might want to consider a wall phone adjusted to desired height.

32. Clean the textured plastic coverings of kitchen chairs, baby strollers, outdoor furniture, and the like with upholstery shampoo. Rinse the surface dry with a soft cloth.

33. Turn a soft-drink carton into a portable cleaning caddy. It will hold two or three cleaners plus a dustcloth and a couple of sponges. If you want your caddy to look good, cover it with contact paper, which also protects the carton against moisture.

Laundry Tips

1. You can cut down on washing and ironing by spraying clothes with a fabric protector on those parts which soil easiest—neckbands, cuffs, sleeves, and other areas subject to heavy wear.

2. Select clothing that requires little care—for example, no-iron clothes that can be run through the washing machine and be ready for use.

3. If you do any ironing from a wheelchair, use a cord minder to keep the cord out of the way so you don't catch it with your wheelchair.

4. Buy no-iron curtains, draperies, slipcovers, tablecloths, mats, sheets, and pillowslips.

5. Close zippers on clothing before you launder them so they won't break or get out of kilter or snag other clothes.

6. Don't iron pajamas, tea towels, or pillowcases (except for a pair or two for the guest room).

7. When washing sheets, plan to put the same pair back on the bed so you don't have to fold them. If you are unable to make the bed, drape the freshly washed sheets over the back of a chair until a family member can make up the bed.

8. Laundry starch protects cotton and linen clothing and household linens from soiling. It restores the original finish to many fabrics so they don't have to be washed so often.

List of Publications

1. PHYSICALLY HANDICAPPED (Booklet)
   Extension Service, U.S. Department of Agriculture, North Carolina State University, State University Station, Raleigh, N.C. 27607.
2. MS IS A FAMILY AFFAIR, Laura M. Braunel, Carole A. James, and Janice D. Stovall
   Easter Seal Society, 2023 West Ogden Avenue, Chicago, Ill. 60612.

3. BEST OF HELPFUL HINTS
   Mary Ellen, Box 444, Minneapolis, Minn. 55440—This booklet contains lots of housekeeping hints, many of which can be used by the disabled homemaker, who, with a little ingenuity, can adapt these ideas to meet his or her individual limitations. It covers everything from indoor gardening to sewing to handy fix-it hints.

There are many books on housekeeping, such as HOUSEKEEPING HINTS by Heloise and the I HATE TO HOUSEKEEP by Peg Bracken. Also, there are many how-to books on everything from minor household repairs to building your own furniture. Any of these may contain ideas you can use or adapt to fit your own needs.

List of Products Available

1. Fashion Able, Rocky Hill, N.J. 08553
   A. Lightweight steam-dry iron—Weighs less than 2¼ pounds. Handle is heavily insulated, easy to grasp with either hand.
   B. No-stoop pick up—Ends "dustpan bending." Easy one-hand use. Folds up to trap dust on way to waste can. Dustpan is 26 inches, broom is 30 inches.
   C. Easy-wring mop—Easy-to-pull lever is 20 inches above floor. Rollers do the wringing, hands never touch mop or water. One-hand operation with handle (47 inches) wedged under arm. 8½-inch head of sponge rubber. Refills available.
   D. Duster mop—Works like broom or dustmop. Washable head; use dry or damp.

chapter five
WHEN YOU ARE THE COOK IN THE KITCHEN

People have to eat and someone has to cook. You can learn to do it and perhaps even enjoy it. It may take a little extra planning, a less complicated menu, plus a bit of practice. The following ideas and suggestions come from people with a wide range of disabilities to help make your role of family cook a more rewarding one.

Adaptions You Can Make

1. If your sink is too low, use a plastic dishpan placed upside down in the sink; place a second dishpan right side up on top of it. Or a rack can be placed in the sink to make it more shallow.

2. For the cook in a wheelchair, the top of a regular stove is too high. One solution to this problem is to place a TV tray next to the stove, using it as a resting place for a pan or skillet while the contents are being stirred or examined.

3. Electric appliances such as a skillet, waffle iron, crock pot, toaster, mixer, blender, etc., can be placed on a low table or TV tray for easier accessibility.

4. Drop shelves are simple to make and provide good work surfaces.

5. You can make a bowl or container holder by cutting a hole in a board that fits over a drawer at a comfortable working level.

6. If you are having some remodeling done, consider adding several pull-out boards at different levels and various work areas. One woman who had a hip replacement, remodeled her kitchen to provide seven pull-out boards at different heights, some for sitting tasks and some for standing.

7. A secretary's chair that swivels, adjusts to different heights, and has rollers is marvelous to use in the kitchen as well as other areas of the house.

Choosing Your Appliances

STOVE

If you can choose a new stove, keep in mind safety as well as convenience. Look for placement of controls, a self-cleaning oven, and other features that are especially important to you.

If you have a stove with controls on top that you cannot safely reach across the burners to turn on or off, there are still some things you can do if you are unable to purchase a new stove or if you live in a rented house or apartment.

There are many small appliances which can be substituted for or used in addition to a stove. An electric skillet eliminates the need for reaching across dangerously hot burners. When you are cooking bacon and eggs or pancakes for breakfast, the skillet can be used right at the table, thus avoiding the need to carry the food from the stove.

Small counter-top broilers are much easier to manage than a regular oven. There are toaster ovens, microwave ovens, and other appliances that roast, broil, bake, and so forth. These can be set on table or counter top within easy reach.

There are also electric grills and waffle irons combined with a grill that can be used on counter top or table. Crock pots that will cook a complete meal are available.

For many handicapped cooks, a microwave oven is easier to use and performs many of the functions of a regular oven with push-button ease. It saves time and cuts down on clean-up chores as well.

REFRIGERATOR

When buying a new refrigerator, shop around for one best suited to you and your disability, such as a no-frost refrigerator/freezer. Select the one easiest for you to reach, with freezer on top, bottom, or side. Consider which way the doors open.

WASHER AND DRYER

When choosing a washer and dryer, decide whether you need a top-loading or side-loading model and which cycles are most important for the types of washing you do.

Handy Utensils and Tools

A pair of kitchen shears, an electric can opener, garlic press, an egg slicer, a baster, and a vegetable peeler are indispensable kitchen tools.

Other useful items are a blender, a portable electric mixer, an electric wok, and a cordless electric slicing knife, which is lightweight and easy to use even with one hand.

If your mixing bowls are glass or pottery, you may want to switch to stainless steel or plastic, which are both lighter to handle and unbreakable. If all bowls are difficult for you to handle, try mixing in a cooking pot with a handle.

Ordinary egg beaters require two hands to operate. A model for one-handed use can be purchased where rehabilitation equipment is sold. Another beating device meant to be used by one hand is the whisk, which is inexpensive, comes in various sizes, and can be found in any houseware department.

GADGETS YOU CAN MAKE

Grater plates may be adapted for one-handed use by building a simple wooden base with a front lip or underlip to hold it in place while grating.

A bread holder can be made by using a four-inch-square board of one-inch plywood. Cover top side with formica and nail four stainless steel or aluminum nails in corners. Excellent for buttering bread.

Planning the Menu

Simplify your menus, especially in the beginning. A casserole that can be prepared early in the day for baking at dinner time is a good choice. The basic ingredients are usually meat, fish, or eggs with potatoes, rice, noodles, or macaroni. If the recipe calls for vegetables, you can use canned or frozen ones and make sauce from almost any cream soup such as mushroom, celery, or cheese.

Dishes such as meat loaf, hamburgers, or frankfurters, are also uncomplicated. Until you master peeling potatoes, why not bake them, boil them with the jackets on, or use frozen ones?

Once you decide what to have for dinner, choose an easy preparation method that requires a minimum of pots. For example, if dinner is to be hamburger, potatoes, and a vegetable, why not prepare a meat loaf, baked potatoes, and a vegetable rather than hamburger patties, mashed potatoes, and a vegetable? You will have only two pans to wash and no greasy skillet.

In addition to canned and frozen foods that are easy to prepare, there is a wide variety of mixes to choose from.

Baking—cakes, biscuits, muffins, cookies, pie crust.

Main dishes—macaroni and cheese, Rice-a-roni, and many more.

Desserts—puddings, Jell-O, pie fillings, and so forth.

Many different kinds of bread require nothing but a quick trip to the oven. There is a wide selection of refrigerated biscuits and brown-and-serve rolls to give variety to your menus.

Fresh fruits and vegetables in season are the best and most economical buys.

One housewife who suffers from arthritis says that on days she feels good or has someone to help, she makes three or four casseroles and puts them in the freezer to use when she doesn't feel like cooking or has unexpected company. She always keeps frozen vegetables, an extra loaf of bread, and some ice cream and cookies in the freezer to round out a meal.

Getting the Meal on the Table

Before a meal can be eaten, the table must be set. Dishes can be carried in your lap when sitting in a wheelchair. Someone who can walk but can't carry things, or needs a steadying base, can use a utility table or a hostess cart.

One wheelchair housekeeper says she sets the table in two or three trips with dishes stacked on her lap and the glasses and cups beside her in the chair. Silverware stacks on top of or in the dishes, and she makes another trip for napkins, salt and pepper, and other incidentals. After a few attempts at carrying dishes, you will be able to judge how many you can manage. In the meantime, you may want to use melamine dishes and not worry about breaking them.

On days when you feel too tired and miserable to do dishes or just want to pamper yourself, use paper plates, bowls, and cups. They come in different sizes and various prices. The small pie plates are great for evening snacks and there are no dirty dishes to clutter up the kitchen.

If possible, have a family member carry the hot dishes of food to the table. If you must do it alone, use oven mitts to handle them, or something heatproof under them such as a trivet or hot pad.

Clean-up Chores

If you have or can buy a dishwasher, it will make dishwashing a lot easier. If not, wash glasses, silverware, and relatively clean dishes first, then do the greasy or heavily soiled ones next. Rinse and stack in dish drainer to dry. If you soak the pots and pans while you are eating dinner, they will be easier to wash. Using Teflon coated pans eases the clean-up process.

Train your family to pick up their own dishes as they leave the table and stack them neatly on the drainboard.

Save dishwashing time: Use your china in rotation so that there's never a group at the bottom of the pile that remains unused. Always take dishes from bottom of the pile, and when they've been washed and wiped return them to top spot. That way none gathers dust.

If you add one half teaspoon of cream of tartar to the water, it will keep the lower part of a double boiler from discoloring.

Egg beaters and potato mashers wash easily and quickly if you put them in cold water as soon as you've used them.

For the kitchen, spray-and-wipe cleaners are great. No messy pads or liquids to handle. Small bathroom or spatter mops can be used in the kitchen to clean counter tops, top of the stove, and many other areas.

Buy supplies and equipment such as brushes, cleaning powders, and liquid soaps in duplicate to make each readily available in kitchen and bathroom work areas.

Casserole dishes that are hard to clean needn't be a problem. Put a tablespoon of dishwasher-type detergent in the dish and fill with hot water. Let it stand over night.

To remove coffee or tea stains from teacups, moisten them with vinegar and rub with a damp cloth dipped in salt.

For a clean range, keep a spray bottle of window cleaner nearby to remove soapy water streaks. Spray it on stove, wipe with a paper towel, and grease disappears, leaving a shiny range top. Dials on ranges come clean with a cotton swab dipped in liquid detergent.

Clean out hard-to-remove sediment that often clings to bottom of bottles or glass vases by filling half full with warm soapsuds, then add a handful of small gravel such as that used in fish bowls. Shake vigorously and watch the sediment loosen.

Cooking Tips

1. A small pizza roller can serve as a rolling pin for one-handed use. Place the dough between wax paper or plastic wrap to cut down on clean-up and to transfer dough to pan with one hand more easily.

2. It is safer to transfer liquids into small utensils with a ladle rather than trying to pour them.

3. There's no such thing as too many canisters, particularly the see-through kind. Use them for opened packages of macaroni or rice, brown sugar, cookies or crackers. If you live where it's damp, a bay leaf tucked in the canister keeps your flour dry.

4. Speed up casseroles or scalloped potatoes by precooking

sliced or diced potatoes in salted water for ten minutes. This will cut baking time by thirty minutes if you're cooking for six.

5. Use large size coffee cans with plastic lids to store cookies in the freezer.

6. When making cracker or cookie crumbs for a pie crust or other recipe, put the crackers in a plastic bag and mash them with a rolling pin. This keeps your counter clean, and you have no problem trying to scoop them up or measure them.

7. You can keep macaroni or spaghetti from boiling over if you add a teaspoon of salad oil or cooking fat to the water before boiling.

8. To prevent burns from spattering grease or steam, use a spatter lid, available from most houseware sections in supermarkets, department or hardware stores. You can also use long barbecue forks, spatulas, or spoons for keeping your hands safe when stirring, turning, or testing food on the stove.

9. A long-handled soup ladle is useful for transferring soups, gravies, or stews from the cooking pot to serving dish. This way you don't have to risk handling a hot pan of food.

10. Make gelatin salads and desserts in a muffin tin. If you have a twelve-cup muffin tin, fill half with grated carrots, cabbage, or whatever you like for a salad. In the other half, add fruit or serve plain as dessert.

11. When using an electric mixer, keep the batter from splashing on work counters or walls by cutting a hole in the center of a paper plate for the beaters to fit through and covering the bowl. Be sure it does not touch the beaters.

12. Store small amounts of leftovers in the refrigerator in small containers, such as paper cups or cottage cheese containers. You can throw them away after use. Cuts down on dish washing.

13. A melon ball cutter is great to extract maraschino cherries or olives from a tall jar.

14. Most salads can be partially prepared ahead of time and kept in the refrigerator until time to add the dressing and serve.

15. For dessert you can use frozen pies and cakes plus many others found in the refrigerated section at the supermarket, such as cheese cakes, brownies, cakes, and cream pies that need no

preparation. Then there's always ice cream, Jell-O, and puddings that are easy to fix.

16. When chopping celery, onions, green peppers, why not chop enough for two or three meals and store them in a plastic bag in the refrigerator or freezer? Saves steps to and from the refrigerator, saves washing and drying the knife and chopping board, and makes another meal easier to prepare.

17. Mixing foods such as salads, cake batter, and mashed potatoes may be much easier if you use a large pot with a long handle instead of a regular mixing bowl. It doesn't require as much strength and a pot is much easier to hold without slipping.

18. When it is impossible to hold a bowl in a tilted position, you can stretch a damp cloth over a saucepan and place the bowl at an angle on top of the cloth. The traction from the cloth will hold the bowl in the required position without support.

19. When baking potatoes, put each potato on end in one of the holes of a muffin tin. The tin makes it easy to remove the potatoes from the oven.

20. A flour shaker near the stove saves getting small quantities out of the canister. Keep salt and pepper shakers nearby too. Saves energy and eliminates extra steps.

21. When boiling eggs, put a little salt in the water and you will have no trouble taking the shell off.

22. Kitchen tools need oiling? Apply a little glycerin with an eye dropper. If any glycerin accidentally gets into the food, don't worry. It's harmless.

23. Goodbye to unwelcome cooking odors. Neutralize them by boiling one teaspoon of ground cloves in two cups of water for fifteen minutes. Or heat some vinegar on the range.

24. Save your large size paper grocery bags. They make an excellent lining for garbage pails and have many other uses.

25. Brighten dull aluminum pans by boiling some apple parings in them.

26. A tri-section skillet heats three foods in one pan for easier clean up. Available at department or variety stores or from mail-order houses.

27. Disposable foil dishes weigh little and eliminate need for cleaning. Available in grocery or variety stores.

28. Breaking an egg with one hand is easy after a little practice. Crack egg against side of bowl, pull sides of shell apart with thumb and index finger, freeing contents.

29. Egg separators, flour sifter for one-handed use, and many similar items are available at grocery or variety stores.

30. Use mixes whenever possible—cake, muffin, cookies, and pancakes.

31. Flour and sugar canisters that can be tipped instead of lifted will make cooking easier.

32. Grocery list preparation—Select articles in small containers or packages for easy handling, or transfer contents of large cans or packages to smaller containers for daily use.

33. Prepare some food fully or partially the day before food is to be served.

34. Instead of wrapping whole loaves of bread for freezing, make packages of two to six slices. This way you defrost just what you are using.

35. Wear a thimble over your thumb when grating vegetables. This will protect both your thumb and your manicure.

36. Oven cooking is easier if you use very light pans or casseroles. If preformed aluminum foil pans are not available, you can make your own by molding multiple thicknesses of aluminum foil into desired shapes and sizes.

37. You can keep a food chopper from slipping if you put a piece of sandpaper between the clamp and the underside of the table or board you clamp it on.

Kitchen Hints

1. Use a table with rollers as an additional work table.

2. Store pots and pans used most frequently where they can easily be reached.

3. A peg board for hanging frequently used items is one way to make them easily accessible without having to take them out of a cupboard.

4. A magnetized utensil holder can keep knives within easy reach, eliminating the hazard of getting cut when reaching into a drawer.

5. When storage cabinets are deep, supplies and utensils can be brought into reach by using lazy susans, revolving corner units, and metal or plastic sliding drawers. Department stores, hardware, and large chain drug stores carry many of the items named above. Rubbermaid has a whole line of these products. The metal or plastic sliding drawers you can find in a hardware or handyman store.

6. Don't use things such as toaster covers. They get dirty and sticky from buttery fingers and are just one more thing to clean.

7. Keep a burn remedy handy in the kitchen for those times when you graze a hot pot or oven shelf. It's no good in the bathroom. As Peg Bracken says, "Who ever gets burned in the bathroom?"

8. When large size containers are economical, buy them and transfer the contents to more manageable containers later. Save small liquid detergent bottles, jars with screw tops, and plastic containers. A covered pitcher can hold milk from a half-gallon container that is too awkward to handle. Buy a small jar of mustard, mayonnaise, etc., then wash it, and save it for future storage of the same product from a large container.

You can do this with cereals, spaghetti, macaroni, coffee, flour, sugar, dry beans, and many other foods you may want to buy in bulk. This idea also works well for things like vinegar, salad oil, and other liquid products you may want to purchase by the gallon or half gallon, as well as for soap, detergents, and other cleaning products.

9. Keep those plastic bags and bread wrappers to use in other ways. They can store items in refrigerator or freezer, wrap sandwiches, slip over ice cream cartons to catch drips, hold cookies or leftover muffins to freeze. You will think of lots more ways they can be useful in saving time, work, and money. Also keep the wire twists or plastic clamps that come on loaves of bread to use again.

10. Make a periodic check of your kitchen. Are there gadgets you seldom use or don't use at all? Either store them somewhere

else or dispose of them. The less you have in your kitchen, the easier it will be to have what you need within easy reach. It is also easier to keep clean.

11. Select the dishes you really use, then store the infrequently used ones in the garage, attic, or somewhere else and get rid of the rest. Of the tools you have, ask yourself if they are the handiest ones available for you.

12. Keep a napkin holder in a kitchen cabinet to store envelopes of sauce, salad dressing and gravy mixes.

13. Various suction, adhesive, and magnetic hooks for attaching tools or utensils to walls without marring the walls are available in department stores and hardware stores.

14. A magnet attached to the end of a yardstick is one way to recover knives, forks, or spoons that land on the floor or slide under the refrigerator.

15. Commercially available double suction bases secure containers well.

16. To make more readily available those small odds and ends such as measuring spoons and measuring cups, buy a rotating necktie rack and screw it to the underside of a cabinet in your kitchen.

17. Convert a kitchen cabinet drawer into an "emergency" drawer. Include in it a flashlight, candles, matches, cellophane tape, adhesive tape and bandages, pencils, note pads, emergency phone numbers, and any other items you think necessary.

Helpful Books

1. YOU CAN DO IT FROM A WHEELCHAIR, Arlene E. Gilbert
   Arlington House, N.Y.—Mrs. Gilbert tells how she does the cooking and housekeeping from her wheelchair. Has lots of good tips others can adapt to their needs.

2. THE WHEELCHAIR IN THE KITCHEN
   Paralyzed Veterans of America, 7315 Wisconsin Avenue, Washington, D.C. 20014—Offers tips on designing or modifying a kitchen for the handicapped homemaker. Storage, appliances, laundry, apartment kitchens, and safety ideas are included.

3. THE ONE-HANDER'S HANDBOOK, Veronica Washam
   Harper & Row, Pub., N.Y.—A basic guide to activities of daily living.

4. BROILERS AND THE HANDICAPPED
   Dept. BH-1, Consumers Union, 256 Washington Street, Mount Vernon, N.Y. 10550—This product-testing organization recently evaluated some models of broiler ovens for use by persons in several broad disability categories. The booklet is available without charge.

5. IF YOU CAN'T STAND TO COOK, Mrs. Lorraine Gifford
   Zondervan Publishing House, Zondervan Corporation, 1415 Lake Street SE, Grand Rapids, Mich. 49506—A MS patient herself, Mrs. Gifford has written a colorful book that covers the culinary spectrum from appetizers to zucchini. Also offers shortcuts and tips to help others face the kitchen range from inexpensive rearrangement and reorganization of the kitchen to inspirational thoughts and poetry.

6. MIKE ROY'S CROCK COOKERY
   Dell Publishing Company, Inc., Dag Hammarskjold Plaza, 245 East 47th Street, New York, N.Y.10017—Many disabled persons may find cooking with crock-type cookers easier than with more conventional cooking methods. Has ninety recipes usable in most crock-type cookers on the market.

7. EASY WAYS TO DELICIOUS MEALS
   Volunteer Services for the Blind, Inc., 919 Walnut Street, Philadelphia, Pa. 19107—The book, published by Campbell Soup Company, is available in both Braille and large print. It has many fine hints and recipes using Campbell products.

8. EATER'S DIGEST—CONSUMER'S FACTBOOK OF FOOD ADDITIVES, Michael F. Jacobsen
   Center for Science in the Public Interest, 1757 S. Street NW, Washington, D.C. 10020

9. RECIPES AND COOKING HINTS FOR BRIDES AND OTHER HANDICAPPED PEOPLE, Imogene Dickey
   950 North Carrington Street, Buffalo, N.Y. 82834—Recipes are given under seven different sections in this spiral-bound book. Includes a list of different tools of the trade, preparation hints, and so forth.

There are many books available for the nonhandicapped that can offer helpful suggestions for cooking and housekeeping. There are cookbooks on casseroles, one-dish meals, skillet meals, crock-pot cooking, and many others. As an example, Peg Bracken's I HATE TO COOK BOOK offers more than 180 quick and easy recipes. You will find a variety to choose from in stores, or you may want to try some from the library before deciding on those you want to buy.

Products Available

1. Cleo Living Aids, ADL Catalog, 3957 Mayfield Road, Cleveland, Ohio 44121
   A. One-hand food chopper—Chops practically any solid or leafy food, raw or cooked vegetables, meats, etc.
   B. Ronson Can-Do—Opens cans of any size and shape. Can be operated with one hand. Portable. Sharpens knives; mixes milk shakes, frozen juices, egg nogs; whips cream, eggs, batters; mashes potatoes.
   C. One-hand peeling and carving aid—You can peel fruits, potatoes, vegetables with one hand, even carve roast or poultry without slipping. Suction cups keep wood block glued to any smooth surface.

2. Fashion Able, Rocky Hill, N.J. 08553
   A. Kitchen shears—Serrated blade opens packages, trims meat, cuts up salads, poultry. Comes apart for washing. 8½-inch blades.
   B. Kitchen brush—Adapted for one-hand use with two suction cups secured to sink or counter top. 23 inches long, with 6-inch bristles 3 inches in diameter.
   C. Jar opener—Will open anything that wears a cap: screw-on, pry-up, or bottle.
   D. Kitchen tongs—For removing vegetables from boiling water, potatoes from oven, and so forth.
   E. Pan handler—Three suction cups anchor frame to stove or kitchen counter. Handle fits between uprights and keeps pot from spinning while you stir. Fits handles 1⅜ inch to 5½ inch high.
   F. Lock-on drainer—Drain food safely with one hand. Locks on easily, grips pan up to 9½ inches wide. Aluminum.

3. H. Hutson, Inc., 2713 South Colorado Boulevard, P.O. Box 1415, Denver, Colo. 80201
   A. Un-Skru jar opener—For those having difficulty opening bottles or jars. Can be mounted on underside of cabinet or shelf and operated with one hand.

4. Nelson Medical Products, 5690 Sarah Avenue, Sarasota, Fla. 33583
   A. Magnetic E-Z Reach—Scissor-like extension with nonslip ends. Saves reaching and stooping.
   B. Aluminum E-Z Reach—Handles objects up to two pounds, yet can pick up a dime or hold a paper cup without crushing it. Weighs nine ounces, adds thirty inches to your reach.
   C. Pick-up tongs—Made of chrome-plated steel, 15 inches long.

D. Hook—Extends your reach by eighteen inches, magnet on tip picks up pins, needles, and so forth.

5. Dale Turner, P.O. Box 726, Puyallup, Wash. 98371
   A. Turn-a-System kitchen shelves—Wheelchair housekeepers may find the kitchen shelves an efficient way to store food. Set consists of eight 24-inch diameter shelves, center shaft, and base.

chapter six
THE GATES OF LEARNING ARE OPEN WIDE

More and more opportunities are opening up to make it possible to achieve your educational goals. Your goal may be a high school diploma, a college degree, vocational training, a means of supplementing your income, or a hobby to enrich your life. The following offers information on many types of programs available, their locations, and where you can find out more about those that interest you.

If you are a high school or college career counselor, a vocational rehabilitation counselor, a social worker, teacher, or member of the clergy, this chapter is a comprehensive reference for reviewing educational options and pinpointing those most helpful for a particular individual.

Getting Your High School Diploma

For those who need a high school diploma, there are adult education programs available in many communities. Many areas have special programs for disabled veterans, such as Veterans Upward Bound started in San Diego, California, some time ago.

The General Educational Development (GED) tests are intended to assist in obtaining a high school diploma. Anyone eighteen years of age or older may take the tests.

GED preparation classes are sometimes offered through adult education courses. A book for home study—*GED Preparation*—is usually available at local libraries. There are several similar books that can be purchased from bookstores.

The GED tests consist of multiple-choice items. Written answers are not required, just select the correct answer. There is only one correct response for each item. These examinations, which can be taken in any order, cover the following subjects:

TEST 1—Correctness and Effectiveness of Expression in English.
TEST 2—Interpretation of Reading Material in Social Studies.
TEST 3—Interpretation of Reading Materials in Natural Sciences.
TEST 4—Interpretation of Literary Materials.
TEST 5—General Mathematical Ability

The tests have no time limit; however, average test time is about two hours. If a test is failed, another form of the test can be taken again after a lapse of six months or after completion of a course(s) of instruction designed to eliminate deficiences.

After passing the GED tests, a person is eligible for the High School Equivalency Certificate, which is accepted by most employers. If planning to go on to college, an individual should consult the school he or she plans to attend for any further entrance requirements.

For information, contact the high school principal, adult education department, nearby colleges, or the library for how to go about taking the GED tests.

Adult Education Programs

Many communities have adult education programs. Some offer a wide variety of subjects including extensive ones for the handicapped, such as career education, employment preparation, body conditioning, arts, and music. Others are geared for the blind, deaf, or other specific needs.

In addition, they may have classes featuring sign language or finger spelling both for those working with or teaching the deaf and for the deaf individual who has yet to master these skills.

There are many other classes available that the handicapped are encouraged to attend, according to their individual interests and goals. The subjects range from creative writing to sewing, from language skills to mathematics. There are courses to broaden your horizons, others to develop a new hobby, yet others to help supplement your income. Most courses are offered for a nominal fee, and many are held in locations accessible to a wheelchair or could be if requested.

The Two-Year College

Two-year colleges are rapidly changing to meet the needs of handicapped students. Some changes made by the schools in California that go far beyond constructing ramps and special parking areas for wheelchairs are doors labeled in Braille, chemistry rooms, biology laboratories, and sewing rooms that have been altered so at least one station accommodates a wheelchair. Some have lowered telephones, drinking fountains, and blackboards in classrooms. Many have installed elevators and automatically opening doors for handicapped students.

A few colleges now have Enabler Services for the handicapped students. Some of these services include special equipment important for the physically limited student, including an electric wheelchair for campus mobility and cassette tape recorders for aiding in lecture note-taking. The latter, for example, would be available to blind students and to those whose physical condition severely limits use of the upper extremities.

One of the major functions of the Enabler Service is to assist students in all aspects of their college life—registration of classes, purchasing books and supplies, orientation to the campus, and overcoming whatever other obstacles that present themselves. Counseling and advising students is an essential part of this program.

There are many programs available at the various colleges for the handicapped student. For the deaf and hard of hearing, many provide note-takers, assistance in obtaining interpreters, sign language instruction, and use of the phonic ear. For the visually impaired, assistance may include reader services and test-taking assistance, large print books, large print typewriters, print magnifiers, tape recorders, talking books, and talking calculators.

Some schools offer special therapy programs including diagnostic testing and therapy for students with speech and language difficulties. These services are directed by a licensed and certified speech pathologist.

Adaptive home economics courses are offered on some campuses to assist the disabled student in nutrition, consumer studies, money management, and independent living skills.

There are also corrective/rehabilitative therapy programs offered through the physical education and athletics division of some of the colleges. The first area includes recreational activities for the physically limited. Facilities are available for archery, table tennis, bowling, trap shooting, swimming, and wheelchair athletics. The second area includes rehabilitative and swim programs for a wide range of disabilities. The exercise and reconditioning programs are therapy oriented. The program works as closely as possible with physicians, medical clinics, and hospitals to develop sound programs. Many people are referred by physicians and medical centers so therapy can be continued after patients are no longer hospitalized. Doctor referral is not required, though a statement from a physician may be needed to tailor the program to the individual's needs. Students may come for these programs only or they may also enter other classes if they wish.

At least one college has a home study program for disabled students who are unable to attend the classes on campus but want the opportunity to complete regular courses. The student is enrolled in a specific class offered on campus during the current quarter and will hear all lectures, complete all course work, do required reading, take exams, write papers, receive grades, and be awarded regular college credit for complete classes.

In addition to offering an associate of arts degree in academic programs allowing for transfer to four-year colleges, two-year colleges offer career programs to students who are seeking immediate employment. Such programs can lead either to an associate in arts degree or to a Certificate of Achievement.

Two-year colleges may offer community services to both the nonhandicapped and the handicapped. These services include the following categories:

A. Noncredit classes.
B. Major topic symposia.
C. Lecture/cultural events.
D. Recreational activities.
E. Community needs assessment.
F. Community use of district facilities.

For the handicapped, the two-year college may offer programs such as Skills for the Handicapped—a craft program offering vocational skills that can lead to potential earnings for those interested in establishing a small craft business. Another course might be entitled A Stroke in the Family: Helping the Stroke Victim at Home. Families of stroke patients have an opportunity in this class to explore and understand the physical, emotional, and social implications of a stroke. They might also include a multiple sclerosis home care course and one on diabetes.

Other classes might include such topics as business, investment and finances, physical fitness, music, dance, theater, writing for publication, personal skills, self-development, science, photography, and history. The charge is minimal and the courses usually don't run longer than six to eight weeks.

To meet the needs of the community, these schools welcome suggestions and requests for desired subjects.

The Four-Year College

Each year more four-year colleges are added to the list of those colleges accessible or partially accessible to handicapped students.

In addition to choosing a college on the basis of academic advantages, you will want to find out whether or not the campus and all the necessary facilities are accessible. Be sure to investigate what supportive services are available, such as a disabled student service center, and so forth. Are there student offices and specific advisors or counselors for disabled students?

If you are going away to school, be sure the parts of the campus you will be using most—classrooms, library, student union, for instance, are all accessible. If some buildings are not, be sure necessary classes are not in those buildings.

How about housing? Are dormitories accessible if you plan to live on campus? If not, is other suitable housing available? Are there enough social and cultural activities available to you? Check on transportation. If you drive an auto, are there parking facilities available both on and off campus?

There are several sources describing the accessibility of various colleges. Some of these are:

A. Brochures direct from the college you wish to consider detailing the school's services and facilities for disabled students.
B. Some schools have compiled lists of several hundred colleges and universities that give information on accessibility, etc. If one of the schools near you has done this, you can go in and look at it.
C. *Getting Through College with a Disability* is a booklet available from the President's Committee on Employment of the Handicapped, Washington, D.C. 20210.
D. Libraries usually have several guides to colleges you can consult.
E. Paperback guides and some hardback ones are available at bookstores. One of these is *Lovejoy's College Guide*, twelfth edition. This one is of particular interest to disabled students because of its list of colleges and universities having facilities for the handicapped.

Whatever school you choose, carefully answer this question: Will it meet most of my education, physical, social, and cultural needs for a full four years?

Financial Assistance

AID TO THE DISABLED (ATD) Those students who qualify for ATD may receive money payments and other needed services from the Department of Social Services.

The ATD program is financed by federal, state, and county taxes and administered by county welfare departments under supervision of the State Department of Social Welfare. In order to qualify, a person must be

- Permanently and totally disabled.
- At least eighteen years of age.
- A resident of the state.
- In need of financial assistance.

Once he or she is determined eligible, the recipient then receives a grant in accordance with his or her allowable needs and with any other income, plus food stamp benefits if desired.

For further information or to file an application, contact the County Department of Social Services nearest to your home.

SUPPLEMENTAL SECURITY INCOME (SSI) SSI is available to blind, disabled, and aged persons in extreme financial need. Eligibility and aid payment levels are based on resources and monthly income. The SSI program is financed by taxes and is administered by the Social Security Administration. All SSI recipients receive Medicare benefits.

FINANCIAL AID OFFICE (Most schools have a financial aid office. Consult the Enabler Service or Disabled Students Office first.)

The financial aid office administers a program of scholarships, grants, long- and short-term loans and work-study employment. A single application is used for all types of financial aid. Incoming students should complete the financial aid section of the application for admission.

VOCATIONAL REHABILITATION The Department of Vocational Rehabilitation is an important tool for rehabilitating physically or mentally disabled persons by preparing them for employment.

A student may be eligible for assistance if there is medical evidence of a physical or emotional disability, if this disability proves to be a handicap to present employment, and if there is a reasonable expectation of attaining employment after rehabilitation.

Medical, psychological, and work aptitude tests are evaluated, a vocational goal is established, and the necessary training and/or schooling may be supplied by the department. During the rehabilitation process, a counselor is available for consultation and job guidance.

If you think you qualify, apply in person or by telephone at the nearest local office of the Department of Vocational Rehabilitation.

COLLEGE WORK-STUDY The College Work-Study Program is an employment program by which the student, particularly one from a low income family, is compensated for the number of hours he or she works for the institution or for an eligible off-campus agency. Consult the financial aid office for more information.

NATIONAL DEFENSE STUDENT LOANS National Defense Student Loans is a program of borrowing, primarily for needy students, in which the student has an obligation to repay his or her loan, at three percent interest within a ten-year period following college attendance.

EDUCATIONAL OPPORTUNITY GRANTS This is a program of direct grants in which the student receives a nonobligatory award of funds, based on exceptional financial need and evidence of academic or creative promise.

GUARANTEED LOANS Guaranteed Loans is a program of borrowing, primarily for students from middle or upper income families. The student has an obligation to repay the loan.

TV Courses for Credit

In some communities television classes are offered for credit by local colleges. Classes appear first at 6:00 A.M., with a rerun in the afternoon and again in the evening, making it possible for people with various schedules to view them at different times.

Vocational Training

TRADE AND TECHNICAL SCHOOLS

In addition to those offered by the two-year colleges, there is a large number of private trade and technical schools that offer training in dozens of skills ranging from watch repair to welding.

Before selecting a trade school, be sure to check with the state or local consumer protection groups, the Chamber of Commerce, and the Better Business Bureau to be sure it is a reputable one.

For a free directory of accredited private trade and technical schools and the subjects they offer, write to National Association of Trade-Technical Schools, 2021 K Street NW, Washington, D.C. 20036.

There may be several trade and technical schools in your community listed in your telephone directory. Again, be sure to check their reputation and study any contract carefully before signing, so you will know the policy of refunding a part of your money if you are unable to complete the course.

Corporate Training Programs

Don't overlook the training programs offered by some of the big companies like IBM, Hewlett Packard, and others. Many include training handicapped workers for employment in their fields.

Two companies that offer such programs are listed below.

1. Joseph Bulova School of Watchmaking, 40-24 62nd Street, Woodside, N.Y. 11377—A vocationally oriented rehabilitation center financially supported by the Bulova Watch Company Foundations and Bulova Fund, Inc. Its purpose is the education and rehabilitation of the disabled so they can become socially well-adjusted and economically self-sufficient. The personal adjustment of each student has been a major focus of their concern. The warm friendly atmosphere combined with an individualized program and excellent supporting services has brought about personal growth to many students. Tuition is free for the disabled. Students work at their own speed in one of the following courses:
    a. Precision Technician Course (average time—eight months).
    b. Watch Repair (average time—eighteen months).
2. C. W. Schmidt, Lift, Inc., 4333 Transworld Road, Schiller Park, Ill. 60176—A six- to eight-month training program (no charge). New cor-

poration organized to select, train, and employ intellectually qualified but physically disabled persons for computer programming and other data processing.

Home Study or Correspondence Courses

A home study or correspondence course can be an ideal way for the handicapped individual to obtain vocational training without having to leave home. Avocational and hobby courses are also available.

WHAT IS HOME STUDY?

Home study is enrollment and study with an educational institution which provides lesson materials prepared in a sequential and logical order for study by a student on his or her own. When each lesson is completed, the student mails the assigned work to the school for correction, grading, comment, and subject matter guidance by qualified teachers. Corrected assignments are returned immediately to the student. This exchange provides the personalized student-teacher relationship.

Home study courses vary greatly in scope, level, and length. Some have a few lessons and require only weeks to complete, while others have a hundred or more assignments requiring three or four years of conscientious study.

Before you get involved, take a good look at your goals. Are you looking for job training? Credits or a diploma? An interesting hobby? It's important for you to be really sure what you want to accomplish.

You also need to take a look at your work habits. Are you able to discipline yourself or do you tend to put things off? If you are a procrastinator, think hard before enrolling in a home study course. Perhaps you could plan to have someone monitor your progress to help you keep on schedule. Consider your home situation and enlist the cooperation of your family.

Once you've decided to enroll, find or make a corner where you can study without distraction and interruptions.

CHOOSING THE SCHOOL

Find out if the school you are considering is accredited. Accreditation assures you that the school meets educational and ethical standards set by the accrediting agency.

The majority of private schools offering home study courses are reputable, but there are some that are not, so select carefully. One of the most important checks you should make is with prospective employers. Find out if they will hire people with the training you plan to get. Ask if they would hire graduates of the school you are considering. Find out if it pays off in a higher starting salary or job advancement.

Before buying a home study course, check with state or local consumer protection groups, your Chamber of Commerce, and the Better Business Bureau for any complaints lodged against the school you're considering.

Send for catalogs from several schools so you can compare what different ones offer. Examine costs carefully since tuition and fees can range from $200 to $1,500. Find out all expenses involved in advance, for example, registration, tuition, and finance charges if you are using credit. You should also figure the cost of any books, supplies, or materials needed to complete the course that are not provided by the school.

Find out the policy on refunds in the event you are unable to finish the course. Also be careful to check the provisions of your contract before you sign. See who owns the contract—the school or a finance company—and be sure you ask about collection policies if you are late with payment.

You will also want to consider the time needed to complete the course and the number of hours needed to devote to the course each week or month.

Once you've considered all the steps outlined above, you will be better able to choose the course that best meets your individual goals.

WHERE TO OBTAIN INFORMATION

For information on college or university extension courses, write for *Guide to Independent Study through Correspondence Instruction* or *On-Campus/Off-Campus Degree Programs for Part-Time Students*. Both are available from the National University Extension Association, Department G-1, One DuPont Circle, Suite 360, Washington, D.C. 20036.

You can obtain a few directories listing more than 125 accredited private schools and the hundreds of courses offered by writing to the National Home Study Council, 1601 18th Street NW, Washington, D.C. 20009.

A sample of some of the courses are listed as follows:

American Automation Training Centers—Courses in automation, data processing, and computer programming.
American School—Complete high school course and college level subjects.
Art Instruction Schools—Courses in commercial art, advertising art, illustrating, cartooning, and painting.
Automation and Training Universal, Inc.—Courses in automation, computer programming, data processing, and drafting.
Bell and Howell Schools—Courses in electronics technology, radio-TV servicing, audio and video recording, and computer programming.
Capitol Radio Engineering Institute—Courses in computer programming, engineering, and college level electronics subjects.
DeVry Institute of Technology—Courses in electronics, radio-TV servicing, audio and video technology, and computer programming.
Gemological Institute of America—Courses in gem identification and appraisal.
International Correspondence Schools—Courses in high school and college level subjects, technology, engineering, vocational trades, business, and industrial subjects.
LaSalle Extension University—Courses in high school subjects, business, vocational, trades, industrial, and college level subjects, stenotype, and interior decorating.
Lifetime Career Schools—Courses in landscaping, floristry, dressmaking, doll technology, and decorative crafts.
Modern Schools, Inc.—Courses in gun repair.
National Drafting Institute—Courses in drafting.
National Education Services—Courses in mobile home park management, dealer salesmanship, accounting, and secretarial skills.
New York Institute of Photography—Courses in photography and photo journalism.
School of Speedwriting—Courses in speedwriting, shorthand, and typing.
Seminary Extension Home Study Institute—Courses in continuing education, Bible studies, Christian history, theology, and ministerial studies.
Technical Home Study Schools—Courses in upholstering, locksmi-

thing, photography, business machine repair, conservation, electronics, security systems, and insurance investigation.

Upholstery and Decorating School—Courses in upholstery and slip covering.

United States School of Music, Inc.—Courses in guitar, piano, and organ playing.

Washington School of Art—Courses in art, commercial art, and oil painting.

From this brief summary you can get an idea of the variety of home study courses available.

chapter seven
TRY ON A NEW CAREER

You are not alone in your efforts to prepare for a job and to find one. Many programs are available to help you, with many experts on hand to counsel you. But even with the programs and the experts, there's one more vital ingredient—more vital than the rest. It's you. When you come right down to it, what really counts is you—your will, your determination, your drive, your heart. So keep on trying. Don't ever stop. Many others have made the grade, and you can too. There are far more career possibilities than most people can imagine. Consider what the following individuals have achieved. Good luck and good courage!

Handicapped People with Outstanding Careers

1. LAWYER A C5-6 quade since an automobile accident interrupted his junior year in college, Jim is enrolled in law school, has married, and is well on his way to completing his law degree.

Harold Krents is blind. His story was the basis for the play and movie BUTTERFLIES ARE FREE. He is a practicing attorney who graduated from Harvard Law School and was turned down by forty law firms before finding the one that hired him. He is active in legal work pertaining to the handicapped and is an expert on the Rehabilitation Act of 1973. He hopes his expertise on legal matters and problems of the handicapped will help open the way for more jobs for the disabled. Krents is married and has a son. His hobbies include guitar playing and singing.

2. DOCTOR   There are several M.D.'s practicing medicine from a wheelchair or on crutches. A doctor in Santa Cruz, California, who contracted polio spends most of his time in an iron lung. By changing his specialty to dermatology, he has been able to maintain an active practice.

Another doctor who is deaf practices medicine successfully. He has a special stethoscope that magnifies sound to enable him to listen to a patient's heart.

3. HYPNOTIST   Paul, who is blind, is a professional hypnotist who has worked with paraplegics, quads, post-surgical patients, and the blind. He has found that hypnosis can speed up the results of physical therapy and cut the therapy time by as much as two thirds. He also works with patients who suffer from chronic pain, helping them to relax.

4. DENTIST   Mark had just finished his first year of dental school when he was in a car accident which severed both legs. As soon as he was able, he went on to complete dental school. A classmate with an engineering background modified all the foot controls on his dental equipment to hand controls. At the time of the accident Mark's wedding date was just three weeks away. The wedding had to be postponed a year but he is now married and has two children.

5. WRITER   Jerry is a quad who earns money by selling articles to magazines. He types with an eraser-tipped mouthstick and an electric typewriter. A revolving book stand which he designed himself keeps a dictionary and Thesaurus close by for easy referral. He can turn the stand with pressure from his mouthstick.

Donna does her writing from a wheelchair and her specialty is children's books.

Other writers dictate into a tape recorder to be transcribed by someone else.

6. ARTIST John, who has multiple sclerosis, is an artist who works from a wheelchair doing most of his work at home. He had to give up his silk screen work when the wheelchair became necessary, and he now specializes in graphics. He's discovered that wearing rubber gloves and putting plastic pieces around his pencils gives his numb hands a better grip.

Darlene, confined to an iron lung since contracting polio, paints by using a mouth brush. She works in watercolors and acrylics. She has sold quite a few of her abstracts and contemporary paintings.

Bill, who has rheumatoid arthritis, is a successful cartoonist despite times when he can hardly hold a pencil. He's done cartoon advertising for many New York firms and has been teaching free-lance cartooning by mail for several years.

Jena does fine quality ceramic work despite having myasthenia gravis.

Bill is a double hand amputee veteran of Vietnam who does beautiful pottery work and has had his work exhibited. His pottery sells regularly.

Joni Eareckson, author of the book JONI, sells greeting cards she paints with a mouthstick. Joni is a quad from a diving accident.

7. TEACHER Bruce, a quad from a diving accident at the age of sixteen, is now a college professor with an M.A. and Ph.D. in mathematics.

Sue, a polio quad, teaches junior high school. For years she was considered unemployable but is now in her tenth year of teaching.

Marilyn, disabled by rheumatoid arthritis, teaches high school English. She has an attendant-companion who drives her to and from school each day. Once in the classroom, she manages her wheelchair by herself, using student help for the tasks she is unable to do.

Ben is a C 5-6 since an airplane crash at the age of nineteen. He sucessfully teaches elementary school and loves working with children. He is married, has an adopted daughter, and lives in a specially designed and built home.

8. ENGINEER David is an engineering supervisor despite being a respiratory polio quad. He was established in his career before becoming disabled so he could adapt his activities to adjust to his handicap.

Don had just finished one year of college when he became a quad. Now he has completed his courses and is a technical draftsman.

Other engineers who are quads include a meteorologist, technician, communications director, and technical writer for an aerospace firm, and many others.

9. MECHANIC Jim doesn't let the fact that he has multiple sclerosis and is confined to a wheelchair interfere with the quality of the work he does at the service station where he works as an automobile mechanic.

Carl, although blind, is an expert in overhauling, repairing, and rebuilding automatic transmissions.

One young man tells of starting a garage with four other handicapped young men. Among the five of them, they have five good arms and one good leg. They became so successful that they expanded their business.

10. PROSTHESIS TECHNICIAN Joe, who lost both legs in Vietnam, became interested in prosthetics (the design, measurement, and fitting of artificial limbs) while struggling with his own. He went on to enroll as a student in prosthetics at Southwest College in California. There are just three two-year colleges offering this course. The others are Cerritos College, also in California, and Chicago City College in Illinois.

11. HORSE RIDER AND TRAINER Dave is a double amputee who works for one of the world's largest Arabian horse farms. He spends about half the time in the saddle and the other half training apprentices and doing administrative tasks. In place of the cues most riders give horses with their legs, Dave uses voice commands and shifts his weight frequently.

12. HOME BUSINESS Roger suffered a broken neck doing a forward flip on a trampoline when he was a senior in high school. He became interested in Amway and developed a very successful home care product business, which he could operate from his home office.

Roger and a friend organized a security firm as a private police agency and they operate both the Amway and police businesses very successfully. In addition, Roger leads an active social life, goes on dates, and truly enjoys his lifestyle.

One couple, both confined to wheelchairs, operate an answering service from their home. They have a switchboard installed in one room of the house and are so successful they have hired two additional operators.

Joan operates a typing service from her home. Her tools are a typewriter and a medical dictionary since she is a dictaphone typist for an orthopedic surgeon. Because Joan is a paraplegic in a wheelchair, she does the work at home and one of the girls from the doctor's office picks up the finished work. She's able to use the dictaphone by putting the foot pedal on her desk and operating it by hand.

Many other disabled individuals operate typing services that do work for small businesses, type student papers, and offer many other similar services.

Patricia makes craft items for sale at home. She is in a wheelchair as a result of polio. She learned to make craft items of felt, ribbons, sequins, pieces of driftwood, and other materials, which she sells through a nearby craft shop.

Fred specializes in high-quality toys for children, which he makes in his home workshop that has been adapted to allow him to work from his wheelchair.

Roy, a polio quad, along with an associate, developed several restaurants that became very successful and were bought out by a large chain. He is now embarked on another restaurant enterprise.

13. HEALTH CARE CAREERS Tom, who has cerebral palsy, didn't listen when he was told he couldn't become an X-ray technician. After being rejected by ten schools, he was finally accepted with the understanding he would have to meet the competition of normal students both in scholastic and technical ability. Tom finally reached his goal and has a job as an X-ray technician. He is married and looking forward to having a family.

Diana is a recreation therapist in a hospital rehabilitation center. She is a paraplegic following an automobile accident. Diana is active in wheelchair sports and she inspires as well as teaches her patients.

Others find success as occupational therapists, speech therapists, counselors, and other health care professions.

14. ELECTRONICS Doug, a C 5-6 quad, is a computer programmer earning a substantial salary. Some large companies sponsor computer training programs for the disabled with job commitment necessary before enrollment. Doug participated in one of these programs.

There are many programs available to train handicapped workers as computer programmers, computer terminal operators, and so forth. There are also electronic assembly jobs such as assembling desk calculators, packaging, and other electronic jobs available.

15. GOVERNMENT JOBS Max Cleland is an outstanding example of a handicapped individual in a government position. Max is a triple amputee as the result of the Vietnam War, and he once headed the United States Veterans Administration.

The federal government employs many handicapped people in a wide variety of jobs ranging from card punch operators, clerks, mail handlers, office machine operators, and many others. Employment is available to the blind, the deaf, quads and paraplegics, amputees, and victims of cerebral palsy and epilespy.

State governments also have a wide variety of civil service jobs available to the handicapped. You can get more information from your state personnel board or local state employment office.

Other Examples of Occupations
1. An electronics assembler who is blind and deaf.
2. A quadriplegic silversmith.
3. A skilled machinist who has lost an arm.
4. A machine operator in a furniture factory who is deaf.
5. A PBX operator who is blind.
6. An accountant who conducts his business from a wheelchair at his home office.
7. A double leg amputee who is a counselor with the Disabled Veterans Outreach Program.
8. A woman who is in a wheelchair is a senior loan officer in a bank.
9. A quadriplegic freelance photographer.
10. A gunsmith shop owner who is a quadriplegic.
11. One state had a governor who was confined to a wheelchair. Politics may offer a variety of possibilities.
12. An insurance underwriter who has MS.

There are many, many more career possibilities in addition to the ones mentioned in this chapter. These may spark your interest or ingenuity.

A Directory of Federal and State Programs

The booklet *Employment Assistance for the Handicapped* is available from the President's Committee on Employment of the Handicapped, Washington, D.C. 20210. The directory lists federal and state programs that provide services to all handicapped citizens who want to be self-supporting. The address of each of these programs is listed in the booklet. Here are a few of the programs.

1. Vocational Rehabilitation—Rehabilitation Services: For physically and mentally handicapped persons who need vocational rehabilitation. This includes diagnosis, counseling, training, employment placement, assistance in payment of medical and related services, prostheses, transportation to rehabilitation services, tools, supplies, and so forth.
2. Vocational Rehabilitation of Service Disabled Veterans: This includes institutional training (college or below), on-the-job training, housebound or sheltered workshop programs.
3. Books for the Blind and Physically Handicapped: Library services to the blind and physically handicapped, including tape recordings,

books in Braille, records, and record players are available through state Library for the Blind or from the Library of Congress. Free of charge.
4. Manpower Development and Training: This includes occupational training for the handicapped, basic education, as well as vocational school and on-the-job training.
5. Employment Services for Physically and Mentally Handicapped: Help for those who are physically or mentally handicapped through federal and state employment offices.
6. Aid to Blind: Financial assistance and medical care for blind needy persons.
7. Economic Opportunity Loans: Provides loans and management assistance to individuals who want to establish or expand a small business.

These are just a few of the programs covered in the booklet mentioned above.

chapter eight
HELP FROM THE PRINTED PAGE

The following selections of books, booklets, and pamphlets cover a wide range of subjects to give some idea of the scope of help available from the printed page. Prices range from fifty cents to three dollars for some, whereas the more expensive hardback books may be in the ten- to twenty-dollar range.

Included in the chapter are sources of large print materials, talking books, or cassettes for the visually impaired or for those who have difficulty holding books and magazines.

For those of you in the health field, many of these books and magazines will be useful to you in working with your patients and some you may wish to suggest they obtain for their own use.

For those in related fields such as social workers, psychologists, members of the clergy, and other professions, many of these selections will be helpful in your work with the physically handicapped.

Booklets

1. EMPLOYMENT OPPORTUNITIES FOR THE SPINAL CORD INJURED, Thomas R. Swories and Richard McCauley; and HANDBOOK FOR PARAPLEGICS AND QUADRIPLEGICS, Alma Frost

National Paraplegic Foundation, 333 North Michigan Avenue, Chicago, Ill. 60601—Both booklets are available from the Foundation. The first one includes chapters on law, applying for jobs, preparing a resume, getting an interview, and overcoming job barriers. The second contains useful information for individuals confined to bed, wheelchair, or crutches.

2. HELP YOURSELVES: A HANDBOOK FOR HEMIPLEGICS AND THEIR FAMILIES, P.E. Jay, E. Walker and A. Ellison
Prentice-Hall, Inc., Englewood Cliffs, N.J. 07632

3. HOMEMAKING AIDS FOR THE DISABLED
Occupational Therapy Department, Kenny Rehabilitation Institute, Publications Department, 1800 Chicago Avenue, Minneapolis, Minn. 55404—A collection of books, slides, and films on many phases of rehabilitation.

4. HOME IN A WHEELCHAIR
Paralyzed Veterans of America, 7315 Wisconsin Avenue, Suite 300-W, Washington, D.C. 20014—Information on ramps, elevators, chair lifts, car shelters, doors, bathrooms, storage floor covering and three examples of plans for accessible houses.

5. HELP ME HELP MYSELF, Carol Green
R.R. 1, Box 3160, 324 Acre Avenue, Brownsburg, Ind. 46112—A large print handbook with self-explanatory illustrations and words covering basic daily living needs. Available in several languages and in Braille.

6. Easter Seal Society, 2023 West Ogden Avenue, Chicago, Ill. 60612—The following booklets are available from this organization. The booklets not listed as free are available for a nominal sum. Contact the Society for further information.

>   VIEW OF LIFE
>   MS IS A FAMILY AFFAIR
>   FIRST AID FOR APHASICS
>   HANDY, HELPFUL HINTS FOR THE HANDICAPPED
>   UNDERSTANDING STROKE
>   APHASIA ACCORDING TO AN EXPERT (Free)
>   STROKE PATIENT REHABILITATION (Free)
>   HOME MANAGEMENT FOR THE DISABLED
>   A STROKE NEEDN'T STRIKE YOU OUT
>   YOU ARE NOT ALONE (Free)

7. REHABILITATING THE PERSON WITH SPINAL CORD INJURY
U.S. Government Printing Office, Washington, D.C. 20402

8. DISABLED U.S.A. (formerly PERFORMANCE)
President's Committee on Employment of the Handicapped, Washington, D.C. 20201

Help From The Printed Page

9. ANATOMY OF OSTOMY
   United Ostomy Association, Inc., 1111 Wilshire Boulevard, Los Angeles, Calif. 90017
10. YOU AND MS and HELP AT HOME
    Multiple Sclerosis Society, 257 Park Avenue South, New York, N.Y. 10010
11. THE WHEELCHAIR IN THE KITCHEN
    "Kitchens," Paralyzed Veterans of America, 7312 Wisconsin Avenue, Washington, D.C. 20014—A thirty-two-page booklet describing suggested kitchen layouts and procedures to adapt kitchens for wheelchairs.
12. Agricultural Extension Service, North Carolina State University, P.O. Box 5037, Raleigh, N.C. 27650—They offer the following booklets for a small fee:
    PHYSICALLY HANDICAPPED
    AIDS TO SELF-HELP IN HOMEMAKING, GROOMING AND CLOTHING
13. SELF-HELP DEVICES FOR ARTHRITIC PATIENTS
    New York University Medical Center, Institute of Rehabilitation Medicine, 400 East 34th Street, New York, N.Y. 10016—Free booklet.

The Arthritis Foundation, Muscular Dystrophy, and Cerebral Palsy Organizations all have booklets and other material available.

Magazines

The following list is a brief sampling of magazines for the handicapped to give you an idea of what is available.

1. ACCENT ON LIVING
   Gillum Road and High Drive, P.O. Box 700, Bloomington, Ill. 61701—One of the best known magazines for the handicapped featuring articles on a wide variety of topics. Includes new products and publications. The magazine also offers a service called Accent on Information. You can send in a search request describing your disability and your needs, which they run through a computer for a list of products and information. There is a charge for this service, but it saves you time, money, and effort. You can also order a complete *Buyer's Guide*, which lists names and addresses of manufacturers.
2. ACCD ACTION
   American Coalition of Citizens with Disabilities, 1346 Connecticut Avenue, Washington, D.C. 20036

3. THE DEAF AMERICAN
   National Association for the Deaf, 814 Thayer Avenue, Silver Springs, Md. 20910
4. DAV MAGAZINE
   Disabled American Veterans, P.O. Box 14302, Cincinnati, Ohio 45114
5. DISABLED USA
   President's Committee on Employment of the Handicapped, Washington, D.C. 20210—The magazine is free upon request. Write and get your name on the mailing list.
6. HANDY-CAP HORIZONS
   3250 Loretta Drive, Indianapolis, Ind. 46227
7. MAINSTREAM
   861 6th Avenue, Suite 610, San Diego, Calif. 92101
8. NEW WORLD
   California Association for the Physically Handicapped, Inc., 5435 Donna, Tarzana, Calif. 91356—Official organ of the California Association for the Physically Handicapped. Their editorial program consists of reporting, advice and counseling, building community understanding, and advocacy.
9. PARAPLEGIA NEWS
   935 Coastline Drive, Seal Beach, Calif. 90740
10. PARAPLEGIA LIFE
    National Paraplegia Foundation, 333 North Michigan Avenue, Chicago, Ill. 60601
11. REHABILITATION GAZETTE
    4502 Maryland Avenue, St. Louis, Mo. 63108
12. REHABILITATION WORLD
    Rehabilitation International USA, 20 West 40th Street, New York, N.Y. 10018

Newspapers

1. NEW YORK TIMES
   229 West 43rd Street, New York, N.Y. 10036—The only large type print newspaper in America. It is published by the *New York Times* every week.

Newsletters

1. ALSSOAN
   Amyotropic Lateral Sclerosis Society of America, 15330 Ventura Boulevard, Suite 315, Sherman Oaks, Calif. 91403

2. THE AMP
National Amputation Foundation, 12-45 150th Street, Whitestone, N.Y. 11357
3. Arthrogryposis Association, 106 Herkimer Street, North Bellmore, N.Y. 11710
4. THE BRAILLE FORUM
190 Lattimore Road, Rochester, N.Y. 14620
5. BREAKTHROUGH
Osteogenesis Imperfecta Foundation, Inc., 140 Euclid Avenue, Apt. 1-B, Hackensack, N.J. 07601
6. Friedrich's Ataxia Group in America, Inc., Box 11116, Oakland, Calif. 94611
7. ON YOUR OWN
P.O. Box 2987, University, Ala. 35486
8. SPINA BIFIDA NEWS
229 Smythe Drive, Summerville, S.C. 29483

Informative Books and Booklets on Handicapped Children

1. ABOUT HANDICAPS, Sara Bonnett Stein
Walker and Company, New York, N.Y. 10019
2. AROUND THE CLOCK AIDS FOR THE CHILD WITH MUSCULAR DYSTROPHY
Muscular Dystrophy Association, Inc., 810 7th Avenue, New York, N.Y. 10019—The booklet covers basic techniques for sitting up, getting out of bed, grooming, bathing, toilet needs, dressing and undressing, eating, recreation, travel, sleep, and emotional needs of children with either moderately or severely disabling muscular dystrophy.
3. CARING FOR YOUR DISABLED CHILD, Benjamin Spock, D.D. and Marion O. Lerrigo, Ph.D.
Macmillan, New York, N.Y. 10022
4. FEEDING THE CHILD WITH A HANDICAP
Public Documents Center, 5801 Tabor Avenue, Philadelphia, Penn. 19120
5. A HANDICAPPED CHILD IN THE FAMILY, Verda Heisler, Ph.D.
Grune & Stratton, New York, N.Y.—The emotional impact on parents is apt to be overwhelming when a child is born with or develops a physical or mental handicap. The author, a psychotherapist, discusses these problems.
6. HELP FOR THE HANDICAPPED CHILD, Florence Weiner
McGraw-Hill, New York, N.Y. 10020—After professional diagnosis and evaluation, special treatments and education are often needed

but hard to find. The author has brought together in one book twenty-five handicapping conditions and tells where to find help through public and private agencies throughout the United States.

7. HOW TO BUILD SPECIAL FURNITURE AND EQUIPMENT FOR HANDICAPPED CHILDREN
Charles C Thomas, 301–327 East Lawrence Avenue, Springfield, Ill. 62717

8. READER'S GUIDE FOR PARENTS OF CHILDREN WITH MENTAL, PHYSICAL, OR EMOTIONAL DIFFICULTIES
Bureau of Community Health Services, Health Service Administration, Parklawn Building, 5600 Fisher's Lane, Rockville, Md. 20857

9. YOU ARE NOT ALONE
Easter Seal Society, 2023 West Ogden Avenue, Chicago, Ill. 60612—A booklet aimed at helping you to help yourself and your child by showing how you, as a parent, can take responsibility for the child and how you can use available resources.

10. YOUR OVERACTIVE CHILD: NORMAL OR NOT?, Sidney Jackson Adler, M.D., with Keith C. Terry
Medcom Press. California Association for Neurologically Handicapped Children, P.O. Box 604, Los Angeles, Calif. 90053

Books on Practical Help for the Handicapped

1. Accent on Living, Special Publications, Box 700, Bloomington, Ill. 61701—The following books are available from Accent of Living:

• BOWEL MANAGEMENT—A manual of ideas and techniques for paraplegics and quadriplegics who have not yet acquired adequate knowledge of bowel training. An opportunity to learn some of the methods taught and used successfully in rehabilitation centers; includes methods to facilitate bowel evacuation, medications sometimes utilized as part of bowel management, program, timing, diet, water intake, etc.

• HOME-OPERATED BUSINESS OPPORTUNITIES FOR THE DISABLED—Gives you important information on getting started in your own home business. Offers practical and workable ideas and reveals case histories of how other disabled individuals overcame the obstacles involved.

• LAUGH WITH ACCENT—A printed collection of the best cartoons from Accent on Living.

Help From The Printed Page

- MAKING YOUR HOME ACCESSIBLE—Tips on what you can do in every room of the house. Gives specifications on ramps, doorways, counters, and so forth. Ideas on how to make adaptations.

- CLOTHING DESIGNS FOR THE HANDICAPPED—Provides designs for men, women, and children with easy-to-follow directions for altering clothing and patterns. Illustrations on every page make following instructions easy. Spiral bound with washable cover.

- ATTENDANT CARE MANUAL—Describes various types of disabilities and the needs of those disabled persons. Provides specific step-by-step procedures for daily living.

- SINGLE HANDED?—If you are a person who can use only one hand or if you know such a person, this book is for you. Includes information on devices and aids, sources for these aids, tips on how-to, and other helpful publications available.

2. YOU CAN DO IT FROM A WHEELCHAIR, Arlene Gilbert
   Arlington House, 333 Post Road W., Westport, Conn. 06880—The author tells how she manages housekeeping, cooking, and care of her children from infancy up. Contains many ideas you will find helpful.
3. WHAT YOU CAN DO FOR YOURSELF, Patricia Galbreaith
   Drake Publishers, Inc., New York, N.Y.—An excellent book for those with physical handicaps. The author has spent fifteen years in a wheelchair and writes a syndicated newspaper column for the handicapped. Chapters on exercises, grooming, baby care for handicapped mothers, cooking, housekeeping, etc. Filled with helpful information.
4. LIVING WITH A DISABILITY, Howard Rusk, M.D. and Eugene J. Taylor
   Blakeston Company, Inc., Garden City, N.Y. 11530—Subjects covered include eating, dressing and grooming, various activities, getting around indoors and out, conquest of the kitchen, and time out to relax.
5. INDEPENDENT LIVING FOR THE HANDICAPPED AND ELDERLY, Elizabeth E. May, Neva Waggoner, and Eleanor Hotte
   Houghton Mifflin, Boston, Mass. 02107—The book deals with the basic problems of home management, clothing, and family relations. Many photographs graphically show how things can be done.
6. AIDS TO INDEPENDENT LIVING, Edward W. Lowman, M.D. and Judith L. Klinger, O.T.R., M.A., Institute of Rehabilitative Medicine, New York Medical Center
   McGraw-Hill, New York, N.Y. 10020—This is a large and expensive book that may be available in your library reference book section. It contains chapters on basic tasks of daily living, sports and games,

clothing, gardening, sewing, recreation and avocation, and much more. It has a bibliography at the end of each chapter and an excellent list of sources for all kinds of products.

7. IF YOU CAN'T STAND TO COOK, Lorraine Gifford
Zondervan Publishing House, Grand Rapids, Mich. 49506—A wheelchair MS patient, the author has compiled 350 easy-to-fix recipes with shortcuts on preparations and tips to save time and energy for those with limited capability. The book is sprinkled with inspirational thoughts and poems to add joy to your work.

8. HANDBOOK FOR ONE-HANDERS, Aaron L. Danzig
Federation of the Handicapped, 211 West 14th Street, New York, N.Y. 10011

9. THE ONE-HANDERS' BOOK, Veronica Washam
Harper & Row, Pub., New York, N.Y. 10020—This book explains in detail with many photographs how to solve many problems of being a single-hander.

10. FOR ME—A "NEW VOICE"—I AM A LARYNGECTOMEE, Stan Kett
P.O. Box 1062, Dunedin, Fla. 33528—Himself a laryngectomee, the author tells what to expect both before and after the operation. Included are such details as how long the hospital stay may be and what the patient may "feel like" both physically and psychologically. Much of the book is devoted to teaching the person to speak in what author Kett calls a "second voice."

11. SELF-HELP FOR LARYNGECTOMEES, Edmund Lauder
1115 Whisper Hollow, San Antonio, Tex. 78230

12. THE HEARING LOSS HANDBOOK, Richard Rosenthal
St. Martin's Press, New York, N.Y. 10010—Aims at helping the hard of hearing to realize that they can get more out of life than they think and not to let themselves be turned into handicapped individuals.

14. WHERE DO I GO FROM HERE?, Don Nold, Editor
DIALOGUE MAGAZINE, 3100 Park Avenue, Berwyn, Ill. 60402—For newly blind persons who have already somewhat adjusted to their new limitations. It is an examination of talking records and of attitudes and images about blindness, as well as an introduction to other blind individuals who have found satisfactory lifestyles.

15. URINARY TRACT INFECTION, Ellen Newman
Box 297 Mayo, University of Minnesota, Minneapolis, Minn. 55455—A well-illustrated, ninety-five-page book.

16. STROKE: WHY DO THEY BEHAVE THAT WAY?, Roy S. Fowler and W.E. Fordyce
American Heart Association—Explains why a stroke alters—intellectual, behavioral, and emotional behavior of the personality and offers suggestions for helping stroke victims cope with the change. Manifestations of right- and left-sided paralysis and the behavior styles of patients so affected are discussed.

17. A STROKE IN THE FAMILY: A MANUAL OF HOME THERAPY, Valerie Eaton Griffith
    Delacorte Press, New York, N.Y. 10017—Valerie Griffith was one of the determined volunteers who worked with Patricia Neal in her recovery from a stroke. She explains the handmade materials and simple activities devised by her that volunteers can use with aphasics.
18. LIVING FULLY, Sol Gordon
    Ed-U-Press, 760 Ostrom Avenue, Syracuse, N.Y. 13210—A guide for young people with a handicap.
19. AGAINST ALL ODDS, Tom Helms
    Thomas Y. Crowell, 10 East 53rd Street, New York, N.Y. 10022
20. HELP FOR THE HANDICAPPED, Florence Weiner
    McGraw-Hill, New York, N.Y. 10020—This is a valuable resource book, divided into sections, each dealing with a specific disability.
21. THE BEST OF HELPFUL HINTS
    Courage Center, 3915 Golden Valley Road, Golden Valley, Minn. 55422
22. USING EVERYTHING YOU'VE GOT, Rev. Harold H. Wilke
    National Easter Seal Society, Chicago, Ill. 60612—Explicit details of ways of coping with the necessities of living without arms and hands by using ingenuity and a pair of well-directed feet and toes.
23. THE EPILEPSY FACT BOOK
    F.A. Davis Company, 1915 Arch Street, Philadelphia, Penn. 19103—Nontechnical, concise publication dealing with epilepsy.
24. HOUSING AND HOME SERVICES FOR THE DISABLED, Gini Laurie
    Harper & Row, Pub., New York, N.Y. 10022—See if your library has this book, as it is a large and expensive one. It covers signposts to barrier-free living, adaptions to housing, kitchen adaptions, bathroom adaptions, organized home services, transitional projects, apartment living arrangements, long-term residential facilities, mobile homes, and much more.
25. GREEN PAGES
    Sourcebook Publications, Inc., P.O. Box 1586, Winter Park, Fla. 32790—Information at your fingertips on sources of items most difficult to find for both services and products.
26. TOLL-FREE DIGEST
    Toll Free Digest Company, Box 800, Claverak, N.Y. 12513—A directory of over 14,000 telephone listings. If you want to find out whether an agency or company has a toll-free number, call (800) 555-1212.
27. HOW TO MASTER TOUCH TYPING STEP BY STEP, Jack Heller
    Special Education Step-by-Step, Inc., 2947 Bayside Court, Wantagh, N.Y. 11703—Adapted to the needs of persons who must use a mouthstick, a head pointer, finger, or toe.

28. HOBBIES YOU CAN ENJOY AT HOME, Lyle Kenyon Engel
    Simon & Schuster, New York, N.Y. 10020—Covers hobbies of collecting, hobbies of production, hobbies of action. Also carries a good bibliography.
29. PROFITABLE HOBBIES HANDBOOK, Alan D. Haas
    Arco, New York, N.Y. 10003
30. CRAFTS FOR THE DISABLED, E. Gault and S. Sykes
    Thomas Y. Crowell, New York, N.Y. 10021—Written by craft teachers who work with the disabled and the elderly. Precise drawings, photographs, and directions.
31. EMPLOYMENT OF HANDICAPPED PEOPLE IN LEISURE OCCUPATIONS, D.M. Compton and D.A. Vinton
    President's Committee on Employment of the Handicapped, Washington, D.C. 20402—Free for the asking.

Books and Booklets on Sex and the Handicapped

1. Accent on Living, Special Publications, Box 700, Bloomington, Ill. 61701—The following books are available from Accent on Living: THE DISABLED PERSON AND FAMILY DYNAMICS, SEXUALITY AND THE DISABLED FEMALE, and SEX AND THE SPINAL CORD INJURED. All three reprinted in one handy reference book. The guide is an anthology of professional observations of those with physical disabilities, what it is and what effects it has on individuals. Among other books, FEMALE SEXUALITY FOLLOWING SPINAL CORD INJURY answers your questions and discusses female sexuality with candor including pregnancy, breast feeding, and more. SEXUAL ADJUSTMENT—A GUIDE FOR THE SPINAL CORD INJURED offers important information for paraplegics as well as for those with other physical disabilities.
2. REHABILITATING THE PERSON WITH SPINAL CORD INJURY
   Superintendent of Documents, U.S. Government Printing Office, Washington, D.C. 20402—A Veterans Administration publication dealing with such topics as the psycho-social and vocational aspects of rehabilitation and sexual functioning.
3. TOWARD INTIMACY AND WITHIN REACH
   Human Resources Press, 72 5th Avenue, New York, N.Y. 10011
4. WHO CARES? A HANDBOOK OF SEX EDUCATION AND COUNSELING SERVICES FOR DISABLED PEOPLE
   Sex and Disability Project of Regional Research Institute, 1818 L Street NW, Suite 704, Washington, D.C. 20036—A textbook for all professionals who deal with the disabled.
5. SEXUALITY AND CANCER, Ernest H. Rosenbaum, M.D.
   Bull Publishing Company, P.O. Box 208, Palo Alto, Calif. 94302—A handbook for cancer patients and their families. Practical and sup-

portive, the book deals with the sexual problems encountered by cancer patients, dispelling myths about sexuality, discussing the effects of illness on sexuality and special difficulties for those with ostomies, mastectomies, laryngectomies, and for victims of cancer of the genital and reproductive organs.

6. NOT MADE OF STONE: THE SEXUAL PROBLEMS OF HANDICAPPED PEOPLE
Charles C Thomas, 301-327 Lawrence Avenue, Springfield, Ill. 62717—The book is well illustrated and discusses general physiology of the reproductive system, genetics, sexual consequences of specific disabilities, sex education for disabled persons, marriage, and family planning.

7. THE SENSUOUS WHEELER
Multi Media Resource Center, 540 Powell Street, San Francisco, Calif. 94108—This book contains sections on human sexual response, sexuality in spinal cord injury, achieving sexual adjustment, the "nitty gritty" of sex, and professional counseling in that area.

Inspirational and Motivational Books

1. THERE IS HOPE, Lucille Gardner
David C. Cook Publishing Co., 850 Grove, Elgin, Ill. 60120— (Available in paperback at Christian bookstores and other outlets where paperback books are sold.) At fifteen Sharon was a pretty, bright, vivacious teenager with great expectations. Before her sixteenth birthday she had become a near-vegetable, stripped by a serious auto accident of memory, health, and her rightful maturity. She lost her past, present, and future. Doctors saw no hope, physically or mentally. But her Christian parents had a vision—and a relationship with a God who cared. The book is Lucille Gardner's story of her daughter's astonishing reentry into a full and useful life, through the love, faith, and persistence of a family that refused to abandon her. It is an extraordinary testimony to a living faith in God through whom all things are possible.

2. WITH TWO WHEELS AND A CAMERA, Bert Kopperl
Exposition Press, Inc., Hicksville, N.Y.—Bert Kopperl learned his craft as an apprentice to the legendary Margaret Bourke-White and later as a photographer for a fledgling magazine named LIFE. On the verge of a promising career, tragedy struck; Bert contracted polio while in service during World War II. With a tenacity as remarkable as his talent, Bert persevered until he became one of Hollywood's best known photographers.

3. THE ABILITIES STORY, Henry Viscardi, Jr.
Paul S. Eriksson, Inc., Middlebury, Vt. 05753—Abilities, Inc., a work center with handicapped employees, operates on a competitive basis with private industry. It was founded by the author in 1952 in

a vacant garage on borrowed capital. This is the account of the day to day economic struggles to keep it a "going" business. The company's involvement in federal projects to habilitate the mentally retarded and its ability to adapt to technological and business changes are described.

4. A MAN'S STATURE, Henry Viscardi, Jr.
Harper & Row, 10 East 53rd Street, New York, N.Y. 10022—Mr. Viscardi tells the story of his life as a handicapped person and the head of Abilities, Inc., and gives the history of J.O.B. (Just One Break).

5. GIVE US THE TOOLS, Henry Viscardi, Jr.
Hill and Wang, 141 5th Avenue, New York, N.Y. 10010—The book relates the history and founding of Abilities, Inc.

6. A LAUGHTER IN THE LONELY NIGHT, Henry Viscardi, Jr.
Hill and Wang, 141 5th Avenue, New York, N.Y. 10010—The story of fifteen men and women, all handicapped employees of Abilities, Inc.

7. THE SCHOOL, Henry Viscardi, Jr.
Paul Eriksson, Inc., Middlebury, Vt. 05753—The book describes the Human Resources School for Severely Disabled Children built on the grounds of Abilities, Inc.

8. LETTER TO JIMMY, Henry Viscardi, Jr.
Paul Eriksson, Middlebury, Vt. 05753—The book gives advice to young handicapped people on problems of adjustment and how to make the most of their lives.

9. SILENT VICTORY, Carmen McBride
Nelson-Hall Company, 111 N. Canal St., Chicago, Ill. 60606—The moving story of one man's courageous battle against aphasia as told by his wife. Written to help other families faced with the problems of living with an aphasic.

10. EPISODE: REPORT ON THE ACCIDENT INSIDE MY SKULL, Eric Hodgins
Atheneum, New York, N.Y. 10017—Eric Hodgins, author of *Mr. Blandings Builds His Dream House*, is a well-known writer and editor. This account of his stroke, his hospitalization, nursing care, and rehabilitative treatment is both instructive and entertaining.

11. THERE'S ALWAYS MORE, Elizabeth S. Whitehouse
Judson Press, Valley Forge, Penn. 19481—Miss Whitehouse is a former editor of children's publications for the Presbyterian Board of Christian Education and later a free-lance writer. This is a personal account of her own experiences after a stroke.

12. MY WINDOW WORLD, Elizabeth Whitehouse
Judson Press, Valley Forge, Penn. 19481—A sequel to *There's Always More*. The author wrote of the stroke she suffered and her successful efforts to become as normal as possible afterward in *There's Always More*. In this book she writes of the exciting and fulfilling life

she has led for the last twelve years as an invalid. Impossible? Not for Miss Whitehouse! "In our livingroom there is a large picture window through which I can see from my armchair the world as it passes before my eyes. It is a wonderful window, revealing a wonderful world, and the people who live in our neighborhood are the nicest people I know." The author, in her inspirational style, writes about the persons who make her life meaningful and of her faith, which has allowed her to see and live in the world through a window.

13. PAT AND ROALD, Barry Farrell
Random House, New York, N.Y. 10022—This is the biographical account of Patricia Neal, the talented actress who suffered a serious stroke at the age of thirty-nine. It is also a story of her husband, Roald, who is to be credited in mustering a rehabilitation program that involved a team of doctors, nurses, therapists, and volunteering friends and neighbors.

14. BORN ON THE FOURTH OF JULY, Ron Kovic
McGraw-Hill, New York, N.Y. 10020—An autobiography of a Vietnam veteran who sustained wounds that paralyzed him from the chest down at age nineteen. He details his path from disenchantment with the war to his acceptance of his disability and the return of his interest in living.

15. JONI, Joni Eareckson
Zondervan Press, Grand Rapids, Mich. 49506—Joni was seventeen when she became a quadriplegic through a diving accident. She tells of her battle with anger, frustration, and depression. She finally learned to accept her condition and is now a self-taught artist who uses a pen between her teeth to draw. She has created a line of greeting cards and prints which she sells in the Christian bookstore she has opened with friends.

16. THE LONG WALK HOME, Leonard Kriegel
Prentice-Hall, Englewood Cliffs, N.J. 07632—A polio victim who went on to gain a wife, family, an education, and a job teaching at City College of New York.

17. A LONG WAY UP—THE STORY OF JILL KINMONT, E. G. Valens
Warner Paperback Publications, 75 Rockefeller Plaza, New York, N.Y. 10019—One of America's finest woman skiers learns what it really means to be disabled and what it takes to climb out of the emotional and physical cage that a serious injury creates. Jill is now gainfully employed. Her story was made into the movie *The Other Side of the Mountain*. The continuation of her life story is told in its sequel *The Other Side of the Mountain, II*.

18. LIGHT A CANDLE WITH MULTIPLE SCLEROSIS, Herb Cochran
513 9th Avenue, Coralville, Iowa 52241—An Iowa farmer used this disability as an advantage to contribute to his community. He tells the story in this autobiography.

19. KEEP TRYING, Joseph Lawrence Marx
    Harper & Row Pub., 10 East 53rd Street, New York, N.Y.—The story of a polio victim.
20. SUN AND SHADOW, Rose Resnick
    Atheneum Publishers, Inc., 597 5th Avenue, New York, N.Y. 10017—Being blind hasn't deprived Rose Resnick of any of the joys of life—or the heartaches. Her autobiography can truly be classified as "inspirational reading," yet it is never dull, never preaching, nor pitying. Rose Resnick has a strong resiliency which has allowed her to bounce back from some traumatic experiences, both personally and professionally. She also has deep compassion, which has made her one of the San Francisco Bay Area's leaders in human potential development.
21. ADVENTURE IN A WHEELCHAIR, Ida Daly with Hazel Flagler Begeman
    Whitmore Publishing Company, 35 Cricket Terrace, Ardmore, Penn. 19003—Written by the sister of this remarkable woman, the book is easy reading with many illustrations. Daly is the inspiration and prime mover for the first high-rise apartment designed explicitly for the disabled. Ida Daly experienced the first signs of muscular dystrophy at age four, and life became increasingly difficult from then on, but she managed to become educated, travel, marry, and paint lovely pictures.
22. TO RACE THE WIND, Harold Krents
    Putnam's, New York, N.Y. 10016—This autobiography, published in large print in 1974, is full of hilarious and tender experiences of a blind person learning to cope in a world designed for the nondisabled. The title comes from Krents's freedom as a child to run down the street, racing the wind, even though he ran into fire hydrants, trees, and telephone poles, so he would learn to be independent. Then he graduated to such daring adventures as driving a carful of inebriated friends, water skiing, and being a catapulted blocker in football. He inspired the hit Broadway play by Leonard Gershe, *Butterflies Are Free.*
23. THE BRAVE WORLD OF HILARY POLE, Dorothy Clarke Wilson
    McGraw-Hill, New York, N.Y. 10020—A fascinating book about a fantastic woman who was stopped in her tracks at age twenty by the little understood disease known as myasthenia gravis. After seven years of time-consuming efforts to converse by alphabetic code, Hilary was at last set free to communicate almost effortlessly by the brilliant brain of Roger Jefcoate and his Patient-Operated Selector Mechanisms Research Project (known in Great Britain as Possum). Hilary Pole now works to aid others in the use of Possum, writes poetry, and travels.
24. RAYS OF THE DAWN, Dr. Thurman Fleet
    Concept Therapy Institute, Rte. 8, Box 250, San Antonio, Tex.

78228—This books offers writings of love, faith, fear, worry, hope, anger, criticism, plus many other subjects that affect our lives. It's a book that will lift your spirits.

25. TESTED BY FIRE, Merrill and Virginia Womach with Mel and Lyla White
Fleming H. Revell, Old Tappan, N.J. 07675—On Thanksgiving Day, 1961, Merrill Womach was a handsome vibrant man actively engaged in his growing music business, much in demand as a concert singer, adored by his lovely wife, Virginia, and three young children. By early afternoon a devastating plane accident badly burned his body and totally destroyed his face, forever altering the direction and purpose of his life and that of his wife, Virginia. It was God who spared Merrill's eyesight and vocal chords from the holocaust, thus rendering his voice richer and fuller than before the accident. And it is God working in Merrill today that gives him the strength to say of his ordeal: "Don't call it a tragedy. My experience has led to all kinds of growth for me and my family—though I hated the pain, I would go through it again."

26. MAKE TODAY COUNT, Orville Kelly
Delacorte Press, New York, N.Y. 10017—When Orville Kelly learned he had cancer, he refused to face the reality that he was dying. Eventually, however, he realized that because of his attitude, he was, in a sense, hastening his death. That is, he was not enjoying what time he had left. Correctly surmising that there were others going through the same ordeal, he organized a meeting of other terminal illness victims for group discussions. Now there are chapters springing up all around the country.

27. DOWN ALL MY DAYS, Christy Brown
Stein and Day, Briarcliff Manor, N.Y. 10510—Christy Brown has cerebral palsy and cannot walk, talk, or use his arms. But by the little toe of his left foot he can communicate word and song on his typewriter. Song is the right word, for he writes with the lyricism of the best Irish writers. The book is autobiographical and is essentially an earthy book about growing up, loving, fighting, and dying in a big family. It is good reading about people you will remember long after the book is closed.

28. EACH DAY A BONUS, Louise Lake
Deseret Book Company, Salt Lake City, Utah—Mrs. Lake is a polio victim and has lived in a wheelchair for over twenty-five years. She tells how she taught herself many of the self-care techniques. She cares for her own home, does her cooking and housecleaning, and makes lovely custom-designed hats.

29. IF YOU COULD SEE WHAT I HEAR, Tom Sullivan and Derek Gill
Signet Books, New York, N.Y. 10010—For Tom Sullivan, being blind has been a nuisance but not a handicap. He is the author of a

best selling book, recording artist, singer, composer, athlete, and television film actor. He is the kind of person who reaches out and embraces life with an Irish joy and sense of humor, and he urges others to do the same—to get out into the mainstream of society, to develop their special talents and to widen their social circles. Written with warmth and humor. His keen senses helped him save the life of his small daughter who had tumbled into a swimming pool.

30. FAREWELL TO FEAR, Tomi Keitlen and Norman Lobsenz
Bernard Geiss Associates, Random House, New York, N.Y. 10022—An excellent book for everyone to read no matter what their disability. If anyone can make you believe in never giving up, it is Tomi Keitlen and her rebellion and fight against blindness. She learns to do the "impossible"—work, travel, ski, swim, live by herself, raise her daughter, and date again. At the end of the book she is considering remarriage.

31. GOD'S MOUNTAIN, James Ashwin
G.R. Welch Company, Limited, 310 Judson Street, Toronto, Canada—Doctor Ashwin, a medical missionary at the time, was attacked by polio in 1955 in a medically ill-equipped area of India. He tells of his struggles to overcome the effects of this disease. Part of his book is devoted to a philosophical discussion of suffering and religious faith, in particular, the Christian faith.

32. EMMA AND I, Sheila Hocken
Dutton, 2 Park Ave., New York, N.Y. 10016—The book is an inspiring insight into the life of a young English woman who lost her sight gradually by cataracts as a child and by age nineteen was completely blind. Emma was the intelligent, loyal seeing-eye dog who guided her through nine years of growth and change. She shares her thoughts and feelings of her first job to her first apartment to her love and marriage.

33. GINNY—A TRUE STORY, Mary Carson
Doubleday, 245 Park Ave., New York, N.Y. 10017—The story of six-year-old Ginny, who is hit by a truck and severely injured, is told by her mother. The injuries included severe brain damage requiring months of hospitalization, followed by years of care at home. Ginny captures the hearts of everyone who knows her and will capture yours as you read about her. Ginny is the youngest of seven children in a devout Roman Catholic family. This story of love, faith, and courage inspires all who read it.

34. VICTORY IN MY HANDS, Harold Russel with Victor Rosen
Creative Age Press, New York, N.Y.—The inspiring story of Harold Russel, who lost both hands in an explosion while on a demolition training assignment with the paratroopers. He is the man who played in *The Best Years of Our Lives* and won an Oscar for best supporting actor. In fact, he won two Oscars, since the awarding

body had decided to give him a special award for his work as a handicapped person before the secret balloting resulted in his winning the regular award for supporting actor.

35. CHALLENGED BY HANDICAP—ADVENTURES IN COURAGE, Richard B. Lyttle
Riley & Lee—Each chapter tells the story of a famous person who achieved success despite being handicapped. Some of those included are Joseph Pulitzer, Charles Steinmetz, Glenn Cunningham, Henry Viscardi, Jr., Harold Russel, Roy Campanella, José Feliciano. An excellent book on courage and inspiration.

36. EYES AT MY FEET, Jessie Hickford
St. Martin's Press, 175 5th Ave., New York, N.Y. 10010—Jessie Hickford lost her sight after she was forty years old. Filled with shock and despair, she wondered how she could ever manage to live a full and independent life without her sight. After being trained to use a guide dog and after Prudence, a golden retriever guide dog, became a part of her life, she learned to do all the things necessary to lead an active, independent life again. Her story, told with humor and courage, is one of trials, triumphs, and, above all, of the friendship and cooperation between a woman and her dog.

37. MERMAID ON WHEELS, June Epstein
Ure Printing, Limited—At twenty-two, Margaret Watkins was injured together with her fiance, John Lester. She was left completely paralyzed from the chest down. In spite of shattered dreams, Margaret sets out to prove that anything can de done. Nine months after the accident, the Lesters were married and today lead a happy and rewarding life. Margaret takes part in several competitive sports; she has completed her degree in architecture; and she runs and cares for her home and three children with great efficiency—all from a wheelchair!

38. FINDING MY WAY, Borghild Dahl
Dutton, 2 Park Ave., New York, N.Y. 10016—A straightforward account of difficulties encountered when the author sets out to do her own work as a newly blind person, showing a rare combination of honesty, pluck, initiative, and intelligence.

39. REACH FOR THE SKY, Paul Brickhill
W.W. Norton & Co., 500 5th Ave., New York, N.Y. 10036—This is the story of Douglas Bader who lost both legs in an air crash in 1931 and fought his way back to become one of the great heroes of the war. It is the story of a man who became a legend in his time.

40. HANDICAP RACE, Dorothy Clarke Wilson
McGraw-Hill, New York, N.Y. 10020—Roger Arnett's story is truly one of victory. Both Roger and his wife, Laverna, are handicapped, and their courage, ingenuity, and deep Christian conviction lead them through their own trials to lives of invaluable service and inspiration to others.

41. CAPE TO CAPE BY WHEELCHAIR, Ernest M. Gutman
    Mitre Press—The author, though physically handicapped, sets out with his wife on a bold jaunt to three continents by automobile and ship in a wheelchair. They explored the peoples and ways of life off the beaten path of tourism; they visited peasants, tribal folk, museums and missions, jungles and farms, mountains and cities, as well as islands and continents. The book is a monument to the positive action of one man to take a major step forward to achieve his desires in the same manner as those without physical handicaps.

42. NO MAN WALKS ALONE, Frank Ellis
    Fleming H. Revell, Old Tappan, N.J. 07675—This is the story of Frank Ellis who walks on a pair of artificial legs, yet who successfully challenged all obstacle courses, survival training, physical training, and evaluation tests given to naval aviators. This is the graphic account of his selfless courage in the plane crash that cost him his legs and of the long persistent struggle to be accepted and promoted as a normal aviator would. He continues to fly a plane and presses resolutely toward his goal of becoming a test pilot.

Magazines and Books Available in Large Print

1. GUIDEPOSTS
   Carmel, N.Y. 10512
2. READER'S DIGEST
   Pleasantville, N.Y. 10570
   A. Braille edition
   B. Talking books
   C. Condensed books
3. National Association for the Visually Handicapped, 385 East 24th Street, New York, N.Y. 10010, or 3201 Balboa Street, San Francisco, Calif. 94121—They have fiction books, many of the classics, and a few modern selections, plus volumes of short stories and some nonfiction.
4. Doubleday, New York, N.Y. 10017—Large print edition of the New Testament of the Jerusalem Bible. The only modern New Testament in 20-point type. Available at local bookstores.
5. Volunteer Services for the Blind, Inc., 919 Walnut Street, Philadelphia, Penn. 19107—They offer free an alphabetical listing of EVERYDAY EQUIVALENTS, KITCHEN TIPS, HANDY MEASUREMENTS, and more.
6. Large Print Publishers, G.K. Hall and Company, 70 Lincoln Street, Boston, Mass. 02111—Many of today's best sellers, adventure and suspense stories, general fiction, biography, current inspirational titles, hobbies, pets, plants and gardening, self-help books, and Merriman-Webster Dictionary are listed. Catalog available.

7. R.R. Bowker, 1180 Avenue of the Americas, New York, N.Y. 10036—Lists 2500 large print books from forty-five different printing houses. Perhaps available as reference book at the library, since it is an expensive volume.

Braille or Talking Books

1. Division for the Blind and Physically Handicapped, Library of Congress, Washington, D.C. 20542—Free recorded books and magazines plus free record players or tape recorders for books on cassettes, not only to the blind but to anyone whose physical disability makes turning pages or holding a book difficult. They also have records of children's books and magazines as well as publications such as *NEWSWEEK* and *SPORTS ILLUSTRATED*. They offer books and other publications in Braille. Free catalog available. When you write for information and the catalog, they will put you in touch with the nearest participating library.
2. National Braille Press, 88 St. Stephen Street, Boston, Mass. 02115—They will tape record any book sent on behalf of a handicapped person, charging only for the blank tape used. They will also follow special instructions. For instance, if a student needs to be able to cite page numbers, they will record page numbers as well as the text.
3. WHERE DO I GO FROM HERE?, Don Nold
   Dialogue Magazine, 3100 Oak Park Avenue, Berwyn, Ill. 60402—This is a talking book for newly blind persons.
4. Choice Magazine Listening, 14 Maple Street, Port Washington, N.Y. 11050—Bi-monthly audio anthology of best writing from outstanding popular periodicals. Subscriptions are free.

Homebound Book Service

1. Homebound Book Service, P.O. Box 354, Fairlawn, N.J. 07410—Send for the catalog of books available. This service is primarily for handicapped individuals who do not have access to local libraries. However, if your library does not have the book, they will be glad to lend it to you. You may borrow books without charge for four weeks. Their subjects include inspirational, instruction, self-help, hobbies, reference, and travel.
2. Projected Books, Inc., 300 North Zeeb Road, Ann Arbor, Mich. 43103—A nonprofit organization which sells ceiling projectors and microfilmed books.

Library Outreach Service

Many local libraries have a Special Outreach Service (SOS) that serves people in the community who, for reasons of health, age, or limited mobility, have difficulty using the library. Free delivery service for books, magazines, paperbacks, large print books, records, cassette tapes, talking books, art prints, and paintings.

Book Cassettes to Rent

Books on Tape, P.O. Box 71405, Atlantic Richfield Station, Los Angeles, Calif. 90071—This is a commercial firm that rents books primarily to businessmen who want to use their time while commuting or traveling by car. The service is expensive but could be a timesaver for the handicapped business person as well as the nonhandicapped. You can choose from a catalog of more than one hundred titles, ranging in tone and period from Daniel Defoe's grim recordlike *A Journal of the Plague Year* to John D. McDonald's considerably breezier *The Dreadful Lemon Yellow Sky*.

chapter nine
ORGANIZATIONS THAT OFFER HELP

No matter what your disability, there are many organizations available to help you. Some you may already know about, whereas others may offer some new possibilities.

Send to several organizations for booklets, newsletters, and other information. The booklets on rehabilitation from a stroke may carry tips that can benefit the person with limited use of an arm or leg due to other causes. The housekeeping booklet from the Arthritis Foundation may offer helpful information for the homemaker with multiple sclerosis as well.

The following list contains the names of national organizations; you can find the local chapter in your telephone book. They may be listed under the name of your city or county, for example, Santa Clara County Heart Association. If you can't find the listing, ask the information operator or write to the national office for the address of the branch nearest you.

Abilities, Inc., Albertson, N.Y. 11705

Al-Anon Family Group Headquarters, P.O. Box 181, Madison Square Garden, New York, N.Y. 10010—An organization for spouses and children seeking to deal with the effects of alcoholism. Has local chapters in most areas of the country.

Alcoholics Anonymous, P.O. Box 459, Grand Central Station, New York, N.Y. 10017—An organization for help in alcoholism recovery and information. This organization has local chapters in most areas of the country.

American Association for Rehabilitation Therapy, Inc., P.O. Box 93, North Little Rock, Ark. 72116—An organization of medical rehabilitation personnel and other individuals interested in rehabilitation of the mentally and physically disabled.

American Association of Workers for the Blind, Inc., 1511 K Street NW, Washington, D.C. 20005—You can obtain information from the address above or you can contact a local organization for the blind in your own area.

American Cancer Society, 219 East 42nd Street, New York, N.Y. 10017—The Society conducts programs of public and professional education along with service and rehabilitation programs at the national and local level. They also publish various pamphlets on the different forms of cancer.

American Council for the Blind, Inc., 15 West 16th Street, New York, N.Y. 10011

American Diabetes Association, Inc., 18 East 48th Street, New York, N.Y. 10017—The Diabetes Association publishes booklets about diabetes and puts out a magazine, ADA FORECAST—a leading national magazine for diabetics and their family and friends.

American Dietetic Association, 620 North Michigan Avenue, Chicago, Ill. 60611

American Foundation for the Blind, Inc., 15 West 16th Street, New York, N.Y. 10011

American Hearing Society, 919 18th Street NW, Washington, D.C. 20006

American Heart Association, 44 East 23rd Street, New York, N.Y. 10010—The Association sponsors many educational programs and offers a variety of publications on heart disease, high blood pressure, and stroke. There should be a chapter near you. If not, write to the address given above for information.

American Legion, 700 North Pennsylvania Street, P.O. Box 1055, Indianapolis, Ind. 46204

American Lung Association, 1740 Broadway, New York, N.Y. 10019

American National Red Cross, 17th and D Streets NW, Washington, D.C. 20006

American Printing House for the Blind, Inc., 1839 Frankfort Avenue, Louisville, Ky. 40206

American Recreation Society, Inc., Bond Building, Room 622, 1404 New York Avenue NW, Washington, D.C. 20005

American School for the Deaf, 139 North Main Street, West Hartford, Conn. 06107

American Speech and Hearing Association, 9030 Old Georgetown Road, Washington, D.C. 20014

Amputee Service Association, 520 North Michigan Avenue, Suite 1504, Chicago, Ill. 60611

Amyotrophic Lateral Sclerosis Foundation, Inc., 2840 Adams Avenue, San Diego, Calif. 92116

Amyotrophic Lateral Sclerosis Society of America, 11520 San Vicente Boulevard, Suite 206, Los Angeles, Calif. 90049

AMVETS (American Veterans of WW II, Korea, and Vietnam), 1710 Rhode Island Avenue NW, Washington, D.C. 20036

Arthritis Foundation, 1212 Avenue of the Americas, New York, N.Y. 10036—The Foundation is a voluntary health agency seeking the total answer—cause, prevention, cure—to the nation's number-one crippling disease. It finances training for young medical students and physicians and seeks to attract more medical workers to the field of arthritis.

Association for the Aid of Crippled Children, 345 East 46th Street, New York, N.Y. 10017

Association of Junior Leagues, Inc., 825 3rd Avenue, New York, N.Y. 10022

Alexander Graham Bell Association for the Deaf, 3417 Volta Place NW, Washington, D.C. 20007—The Association provides information services for parents, libraries, hospitals, and others who are interested in the hearing impaired. They also publish numerous books and brochures about hearing impairment.

Biofeedback, Etc., 412 Woodward Boulevard, Pasadena, Calif. 91107—A paraplegic who wrote of her experiences with Biofeedback has started a newsletter. She has been in contact with many others who are trying Biofeedback and various methods of controlling movement and pain.

Boy Scouts of America, Scouting for the Handicapped Division, North Brunswick, N.J. 08902—The Scouting for the Handicapped Program for both girls and boys is a special program whose aim is to have handicapped youngsters included in the regular troop activities of both groups as much as possible.

Braille Institute of America, Inc., 741 North Vermont Avenue, Los Angeles, Calif. 90029

Braille Technical Press, Inc., 980 Waring Avenue, New York, N.Y. 10469

California Association for Neurologically Handicapped Children, P.O. Box 20013, San Diego, Calif. 92120, or P.O. Box 6478, San Jose, Calif. 95150

Cancer Care, Inc., 1 Park Avenue, New York, N.Y. 10016

Cancer Patients Anonymous, 48 Cedar Valley Lane, Huntington, N.Y. 11743

CHAP (Children Have a Potential), Forrestal Building, 1000 Independence Avenue SW, Washington, D.C. 20314—An official Air Force program designed to make available, when possible, all the services required to assist Air Force families throughout the world who have children with a physical, emotional, or intellectual handicap. The assistance may be in the form of counseling and referral concerning medical, educational, or recreational services, special assignment consideration, and/or financial assistance.

Children's Bureau, Office of Child Development, Department of Education, P.O. Box 1182, Washington, D.C. 20013

Comeback, Inc., 16 West 46th Street, New York, N.Y. 10036

Committee to Combat Huntington's Disease, 250 West 57th Street, New York, N.Y. 10019—Organized by Marjorie Guthrie after the death of her husband, Woody Guthrie, the famous folk singer, to reach other families with HD and to promote research into its cure and treatment. Informative pamphlets and a newsletter are available without charge.

Committee for the Handicapped, People to People Program, LaSalle Building, Suite 610, Connecticut Avenue and L Street, Washington, D.C. 20036—They publish a directory of organizations interested in the handicapped.

Council for Exceptional Children, National Education Association, 1201 16th Street NW, Washington, D.C. 20036

Deafness Research Foundation, 310 Lexington Avenue, New York, N.Y. 10016

Disabled American Veterans, 3725 Alexander Pike, Cold Spring, Ky. 41076—DAV's paramount objective is to promote the welfare of the service-connected disabled veteran and his dependents and to provide a service program to assist them in their claims before the Veterans Administration and other government agencies.

Federation of the Handicapped, Inc., 111 West 14th Street, New York, N.Y. 10011

Friedreich's Ataxia Group in America, Inc., P.O. Box 1116, Oakland, Calif. 94611

Girl Scouts of America, Scouting for Handicapped Girls, 830 3rd Avenue, New York, N.Y. 10022—The Scouting for the Handicapped Program for both girls and boys is a special program whose aim is to have handicapped youngsters included in the regular troop activities of both groups as much as possible.

Gallaudet College, 7th Street and Florida Avenue NE, Washington, D.C. 20002—The world's only liberal arts college for the deaf whose purpose is to afford its students the intellectual development that can be acquired through a study of the liberal arts and sciences.

Goodwill Industries of America, 1913 N Street NW, Washington, D.C. 20036—An organization that has sheltered workshops for the disabled.

Hadley School for the Blind, 700 Elm Street, Winnetka, Ill. 60093

HEARING-EAR DOGS

Dogs are now being trained to aid the deaf or hard of hearing. It takes four to six months to train these dogs to respond to alarm clocks, smoke and fire alarms, doorbells, crying babies, and other essential sounds. On the street, these dogs let their owners know about approaching traffic, and they can be trained to pick up objects their owners accidentally drop. Almost any bright dog, regardless of size, can become a hearing-ear dog.

Colorado, Connecticut, and California have already passed laws giving hearing-ear dogs the same privileges accorded seeing-eye dogs. They are allowed on public transportation and other places where dogs are usually prohibited. Here is a list of training centers.

>Hearing Dog Program, 5351 S. Roslyn Street, Engelwood, Colo. 80110
>
>Hearing-Ear Dog Program, Holliston Junior College, Lenox Campus, 45 West Street, Lenox, Mass. 02140
>
>Applegate Behavior Station, 13260 Highway 238, Jacksonville, Oreg. 97530
>
>Canine Companions, 14238 Briarwood Terrace, Rockville, Md. 20853
>
>Hearing-Ear Dog Program, Bryant Hill Farm, 76 Bryant Road, Jefferson, Mass. 01522

Heart Information Center, National Heart Institute, Bethesda, Md. 20014

Homebound Book Service, P.O. Box 354, Fairlawn, N.J. 07410—A free lending service of books about handicapped persons.

Howe Press, Perkins School for the Blind, 175 North Beacon Street, Watertown, Mass. 02172—Offers writing and reading aids for the blind.

ICD Rehabilitation and Research Center (Formerly Institute for the Crippled and Disabled), 340 East 24th Street, New York, N.Y. 10010—An international organization dedicated to the improvement of the condition of handicapped persons through rehabilitation treatment, training, research, and professional education.

International Association of Laryngectomees, 279 East 42nd Street, New York, N.Y. 10017—The Association is made up of the Lost Chord and New Voice Clubs who have contact with approximately 16,000 laryngectomees.

International Association of Rehabilitation Facilities, Inc., 5530 Wisconsin Avenue, Room 955, Washington, D.C. 20015—The Association encompasses 700 medically oriented rehabilitation centers and sheltered workshops.

International Cystic Fibrosis (Mucoviscidosis) Association, 521 5th Avenue, New York, N.Y. 10017

International Handicapped NET, P.O. Box 8, San Gabriel, Calif. 91778—IHN's chief objective is to promote international goodwill among radio amateurs who are handicapped. NET operations are on 14287 KHZ Monday through Friday at 1600 GMT or an hour earlier when daylight savings time is in force, with the NET operating for two hours.

Junior National Association of the Deaf, Galludet College, 7th Street and Florida Avenue NE, Washington, D.C. 20002—A national student organization whose purpose is to motivate all deaf young people to utilize their potential and to bring them into the mainstream of American life.

Lexington School for the Deaf, 904 Lexington Avenue, New York, N.Y. 10019

Library of Congress, Division for the Blind and Physically Handicapped, Washington, D.C. 20542—A national program to provide free library service to persons who are unable to read standard print materials because of visual or physical impairment. Books and magazines in record and Braille formats are produced and distributed to a network of over 140 cooperating regional and subregional libraries throughout the United States, which provide direct service to eligible persons.

Muscular Dystrophy Association of America, Inc., 810 Seventh Avenue, New York, N.Y. 10019—A voluntary health organization which fosters research seeking cures or effective treatments for muscular dystrophy and related neuromuscular diseases. Publishes booklets with patient and community information.

Myasthenia Gravis Foundation, Inc., 2 East 103rd Street, New York, N.Y. 10029—A nonprofit organization for the advancement of rehabilitation and education in MG, which publishes a handbook for MG patients and a newsletter entitled MG CONQUEST.

National Accreditation Council for Agencies Serving the Blind and Visually Handicapped, 84 5th Avenue, Suite 501, New York, N.Y. 10011

National Aid to Visually Handicapped, 3201 Balboa, San Francisco, Calif. 94121—Publishes large print books for the blind.

National Association for Brain Injured Children, 1617 East 7th Street, Brooklyn, N.Y. 11215

National Association of the Deaf, 814 Thayer Avenue, Silver Springs, Md. 20910—Founded in 1880, the Association serves as a clearinghouse for information relating to deafness. A free list of publications is available.

National Association for Retarded Children, Inc., 420 Lexington Avenue, New York, N.Y. 10017

National Association of the Physically Handicapped, Inc., 6473 Grandville Avenue, Detroit, Mich. 48228

National Association of Sheltered Workshops and Homebound Programs, 1522 K Street NW, Washington, D.C. 20006

National Cystic Fibrosis Research Foundation, 521 5th Avenue, New York, N.Y. 10017

National Disabled Law Officers Association, Inc., 75 New Street, Nutley, N.J. 07110—The aim of the Association is to further the employment of the estimated 5,000 disabled law officers in the country and to effect legislation to provide more and better benefits. Operating without dues, the organization offers an information service which includes sharing the names and addresses of other disabled lawmen.

National Easter Seal Society for Crippled Children and Adults, 2023 West Odgen Avenue, Chicago, Ill. 60612—The National Easter Seal Society for Crippled Children and Adults is the largest service agency concerned directly with meeting the needs of the disabled. It operates more than 2,500 programs for the benefit of all disabled throughout the fifty states, Puerto Rico, and the District of Columbia. The programs include rehabilitation and treatment centers, sheltered workshops, home employment services, and residential and day camps. The service programs differ from place to place, except for a basic program of information, referral, and follow-up, which assures the handicapped individual and his or her family of guidance in the use of all resources available to them. Any parent of a handicapped child who has been bewildered by the maze of agencies and services, not knowing where to turn to for help, will certainly realize the value of the Society's basic program.

National Epilepsy League, 203 North Wabash Avenue, Chicago, Ill. 60601

National Federation for the Blind, 218 Randolph Hotel Building, Des Moines, Iowa 50309

National Foundation for Eye Research, B.F. Keith Building, Suite 1130, Cleveland, Ohio 44115

National Foundation/March of Dimes, 1275 Mamaroneck Avenue, White Plains, N.Y. 10605—The Foundation's goal is the prevention of birth defects. Publishes pamphlets, booklets, and audiovisual materials for the general public on the prevention of birth defects.

National Foundation for Neuromuscular Diseases, Inc., 150 West 57th Street, New York, N.Y. 10018

National Inconvenienced Sportsperson's Association, 3778 Walnut Avenue, Carmichael, Calif. 95608—A nationwide organization providing sports and recreational opportunities for the deaf, blind, neurologically damaged, and amputees.

National Industries for the Blind, 1455 Broad Street, Bloomfield, N.J. 07003—Organized for the purpose of promoting gainful employment for all those blind and multi-handicapped persons who can and want to work. They have workshops in thirty-five states, the District of Columbia, and Puerto Rico.

National Multiple Sclerosis Society, 257 Park Avenue South, New York, N.Y. 10010—They have programs at local, national, and international levels working to coordinate, stimulate, and support research to determine the cause, prevention, alleviation, and cure of multiple sclerosis and related diseases of the central nervous system.

National Paraplegia Foundation, 333 North Michigan Avenue, Chicago, Ill. 60601—Founded in 1948 by the Paralyzed Veterans of America, the Foundation is concerned with both research for a cure and the continuing care and total environment of those disabled by spinal cord injuries. Its informative bi-monthly publication, PARAPLEGIC LIFE, is free to members. A comprehensive list of publications relating to spinal cord injury is available.

National Rehabilitation Association, 1522 K Street NW, Washington, D.C. 20005—The NRA is dedicated to the rehabilitation of all physically handicapped persons and strives to increase opportunities for handicapped persons to become self-sufficient, self-supporting, and contributing members of their communities. Each state has its own vocational rehabilitation department.

National Recreation and Park Association and National Therapeutic Recreation Society, 8 West 8th Street, New York, N.Y. 10011—Consulting service for the ill and handicapped.

National Tuberculosis Association, 1740 Broadway, New York, N.Y. 10019—Offers information on TB and other respiratory diseases. They have several helpful booklets available.

National Vocational Guidance Association, Inc., 1605 New Hampshire Avenue NW, Washington, D.C. 20009

National Wheelchair Athletic Association, Bulova School of Watchmaking, 40-24 62nd Street, Woodside, N.Y. 11377

New York Association for the Blind, 111 East 59th Street, New York, N.Y. 10022

Open Doors for the Handicapped, 1013 Brintell Street, Pittsburgh, Penn. 15201

Osteogenesis Imperfecta Foundation, Inc., 1231 May Court, Burlington, N.C. 27215—Its purpose is to fund research and to exchange information between OI patients and their families. Its quarterly publication BREAKTHROUGH contains sections on penpals, successful careers, equipment information, and information on its nationwide chapters.

Our Way, 4303 Bradley Lane, Chevy Chase, Md. 20015—A nonprofit group concerned with the problems of the disabled in general and specifically with those who may be single-handed.

Paralyzed Veterans of America, 432 Park Avenue South, New York, N.Y. 10016—An organization of veterans who have served honorably in the armed forces and incurred injury or disease affecting the spinal cord. They are concerned with veterans and nonveterans.

Parkinson's Disease Foundation, Inc., 710 West 168th Street, New York, N.Y. 10032

Paraplegics Manufacturing Company, Inc., 304 North York Road, Bensenville, Ill. 60106—The company operates primarily as a subcontractor to major manufacturers in the assembly and fabrication of electronic and electro-mechanical products and devices. Organized for the purpose of employing paraplegics and other physically handicapped persons.

Perkins School for the Blind, 175 North Beacon Street, Watertown, Mass. 02172—The school is concerned with the education of blind and deaf-blind pupils and training programs for teachers in that field, as well as with guidance in individual daily living skills for the young blind and deaf-blind adults.

Placement and Referral Center for Handicapped Students, 131 Livingston Street, Brooklyn, N.Y. 11201—The Center provides job placement, career counseling, follow-up, and referral to social, rehabilitation, and education agencies and maintains liaison with business and labor unions.

President's Committee on Employment of the Handicapped, 20th and L Streets NW, Washington, D.C. 20210—Established in 1947 by the President of the United States, every U.S. president since then has given his personal and active support to full employment opportunities for the physically and mentally handicapped. The Committee is composed of more than 600 volunteer organizations and individuals representing business, industry, labor, and many other concerned groups.

Prosthetic and Sensory Aids Service, Veterans Administration, 252 7th Avenue, New York, N.Y. 10001

Rehabilitation International USA, 17 East 45th Street, New York, N.Y. 10017—RIUSA was founded to offer international services to the US rehabilitation community as well as for the benefit of the handicapped worldwide. It has agencies in more than 60 countries devoted to helping the disabled.

Recordings for the Blind, 215 East 58th Street, New York, N.Y. 10022

Superintendent of Documents, U.S. Government Printing Office, Washington, D.C. 20025—Write for any booklets or pamphlets on any subject desired, or send for their listing of those available dealing with disability.

Spina Bifida Association of America, 104 Festone Avenue, New Castle, Del. 19720

Stroke Clubs of America, 805 12th Street, Galveston, Tex. 77550

United Cerebral Palsy Association, Inc., 66 East 34th Street, New York, N.Y. 10016—Voluntary health organization dedicated to a continuing overall attack on cerebral palsy and seeking to find solutions to the multiple problems of its victims.

United Ostomy Association, Inc., 1111 Wilshire Boulevard, Los Angeles, Calif. 90017—Founded in 1962, its purpose is to disseminate information to persons who have lost the normal function of their bowel or bladder necessitating colostomy, ileostomy, or urinary diversion surgery. It publishes care and management manuals and the OSTOMY QUARTERLY.

U.S. Department of Health, Children's Bureau, Office of Child Development, P.O. Box 1182, Washington, D.C. 20013

University of Illinois, Rehabilitation Education Center, Oak and Stadium Drive, Champaign, Ill. 61820

Vocational Rehabilitation Administrator, U.S. Department of Health, Washington, D.C. 20201

Women's Bureau, U.S. Department of Labor, Washington, D.C. 20210

Many areas have local clubs for stroke victims, mastectomy, laryngectomy, or colostomy patients. These clubs can offer help in coping and support to both the patients and their families. It can be comforting to know that other people are faced with the same difficulties and are working together for solutions. They may be sponsored by the American Cancer Society, Heart Association, or a similar organization.

Find out what local organizations are doing and join those that appeal to you. For instance, Expanding Horizons in San Jose, California, was founded by Gary Capen, a recreational therapist whose goal is to help the handicapped make their lives richer and more rewarding.

Another organization is the California Association of the Physically Handicapped, Inc., which has chapters in various counties throughout the state of California. Its purpose is to obtain for the handicapped person the same items of everyday life that are enjoyed by the able-bodied. It is active at the state level in working for legislation to benefit the handicapped. The members attend local meetings and participate in various recreational programs. There is also an annual CAPH convention, where new products and services are shown and speakers on pertinent topics are featured. Why not find out if your state has a similar organization?

The service organizations such as Elks, Lions, Kiwanis, Rotary, Sertoma, and others often sponsor various programs for the handicapped. These may vary from one locale to another, but you can find out what they offer in your own area by contacting the local clubs.

chapter ten
STRETCHING YOUR DOLLARS

Many of the following suggestions are well known while others may not be so familiar. This chapter is intended to list as many options as possible for increased income or special services needed.

Social Security Disability

If you think you qualify for disability, discuss it with your doctor. It is especially difficult for individuals with arthritis, multiple sclerosis, and other progressive diseases to know at what point they are eligible to receive Social Security Disability. You will usually have to take the initiative yourself, as many times you are the only one completely aware of your changing limitations.

Public Assistance

A. Aid to the blind.
B. Aid to permanently and totally disabled.
C. Under the Adult Homemaker Service Division of your local department you may be able to qualify for homemaker service without being on welfare.

Supplemental Security Income (SSI)

SSI checks go to people who are blind or disabled and have little or no income and who do not own much in the way of resources. You can get SSI checks even while you are working or if you are getting a small Social Security check or some other pension, if your earnings aren't too high. In most states people eligible for SSI also qualify automatically for Medicaid. Contact your local Social Security Office for further information.

Voluntary Organizations

The Easter Seal Society for Crippled Children and Adults provides the following aid:

A. Equipment loan—emergency hospital equipment is available for loan for as long as it is needed. They will also work with other health agencies to provide such services.
B. Equipment purchase—they will purchase orthopedic shoes, braces, and other special orthopedic equipment on an individual case basis.
C. Other services—they will purchase services, such as physical therapy, speech therapy, special education, and others on an individual basis.

There is no charge to the disabled for the services noted above. For information, contact your local Easter Seal Society or write to National Easter Seal Society, 2023 West Ogden Avenue, Chicago, Ill. 60612.

In some communities the local Heart Association will help with equipment and special services.

Special Income Tax Deductions

Disabled individuals are entitled to special income tax deductions in the areas of home improvements, medical expenses, and business expenses.

A. HOME IMPROVEMENTS   Internal Revenue Service rules clearly allow deductions for special equipment installed for medical reasons, such as an elevator ramp for someone in a wheelchair. Whether you own or rent, you can claim the entire cost of detachable equipment. Anything that adds to the value of the home requires closer scrutiny of the tax rules, and even if you can't deduct the cost of some additions, you might still be able to deduct repairs and maintenance. Be sure to get a written statement from your doctor that the equipment is needed for medical reasons and keep all your bills, receipts, and cancelled checks in case of an IRS audit.

B. MEDICAL EXPENSES Don't overlook the mileage to and from the doctors' offices or hospitals as part of your deductible medical expenses. For the sight-impaired, be sure to check on purchase of Braille books or supplies. In some cases the difference in cost of a regular book and one printed in Braille may be considered "necessary for the alleviation of a physical defect" and therefore a medical deduction. You can request a copy from the IRS of their publication, DEDUCTIONS FOR MEDICAL AND DENTAL EXPENSES.

C. BUSINESS EXPENSES If a disabled individual travels on business and he requires someone to travel with him or her, the expenses of the other person are deductible as business expenses. the services provided while traveling are the same as that required for nontravel, they would be medical deductions rather than business ones. Again, check with the IRS or whoever prepares your income tax. If a blind worker requires a reader's services full or part time in order to perform his or her duties on the job, this would be a business expense.

Veteran's Benefits

The Veterans Administration and other federal and state agencies conduct many programs that provide substantial benefits and services to disabled veterans, especially to those veterans who are severely disabled. Among these benefits and services are

- Comprehensive health and medical care, including hospitalization, out-patient medical treatment, out-patient dental treatment, and the provision of prosthetic appliances.

- Disability compensation and disability pension.
- Nursing home care and domiciliary care.
- Electronic and mechanical aids and guide dogs to blinded veterans, including payment of the cost of training the veteran in using the dog.
- Vocational rehabilitation and educational training.
- Specially adapted housing assistance for the severely disabled veteran having distinctive housing needs, such as wide doors to accommodate a wheelchair, ramps instead of steps, oversized and specially equipped bathrooms, and so forth.
- Funds for the purchase of an automobile and necessary adaptive equipment.
- Mortgage insurance, property tax abatement, and commissary and exchange privileges.
- Special allowances for aides and attendants if these services are required.
- Special consideration and services in job placement.

Small Business Loans

SCORE (Service Corps of Retired Executives) is a retired businessmen's association that helps small businesses get started. Sometimes they help by approving a proposed business and getting information from banks that help people qualify for a loan through the Small Business Administration.

One disabled couple was able to buy an answering service that they could operate from their home. After many discouraging encounters with banks and other loan sources, SCORE was able to help them. Inquire at your bank or local Small Business Administration office for further information.

Housing Alternatives

Until recently there were few alternatives to nursing homes for the severely disabled. Now there is an increasing number of other housing options.

Several communities are building or buying and altering apartment houses for groups of handicapped people. Some are run similar to retirement homes where there is a nurse on call twenty-four hours and meals are in a community dining room. Others are small individual apartments and the person has attendant care as needed. Others are group homes where several handicapped individuals help each other with the cooking, cleaning, and necessary chores, each sharing part of the rent and expenses.

Housing developers now design and build private residences with wider doors, ramps, and kitchens and bathrooms designed to meet individual needs.

Some colleges have used mobile homes as disabled student housing. It's also a good possibility for a married couple, with a few changes or adaptions to make it accessible.

Mobile Homes for the Handicapped

There is now a mobile home built specifically for wheelchair living. The kitchen and bathroom counters are only thirty-two inches high; stove and ovens are set at a comfortable height; sinks are front-accessible, and cupboards are at a height you can reach. All doors are three feet wide; closets and showers are roll-in, and grab bars are standard in all bathrooms. It is called "The Independence" and is offered in one- and two-bedroom models.

They also have special classroom models and a four-bedroom, four-bath dormitory unit. A free brochure is available from Coast Mobile Home Sales, 23639 Arlington Avenue, Torrance, Calif. 90501 or 12505 Beach Boulevard, Garden Grove, Calif. 92641.

Insurance

According to Ron Mincer's "Insurance Corner" in NEW WORLD, the CAPH (California Association for the Physically Handicapped) monthly, there is progress being made in obtaining insurance for those who previously had been turned down by other companies. Anyone who has been turned down for health, life, or automobile insurance by any insurance company for any reason should contact Ed Wicander and let him know what is needed. Write to Ed Wicander, 1546 Monte Mar Road, Vista, Calif. 92083.

Mail-Order Shopping

Mail-order shopping can be a real help to the handicapped shopper. A few suggestions to keep you from getting cheated are as follows:

1. Never send cash through the mail. Always use a check or money order so you can have a record of when you sent your order and when the company received it.

2. Make sure there is a guaranteed delivery date. If you are ordering for a special date, you want to make sure the item is received on time.

3. Find out the company's policy on returns. If it is not mentioned in the ad, write the company first and ask what it is.

4. Beware of exaggerated claims on the product or price. Look the ad over carefully. If it seems too good to be true, it usually is.

5. Keep a record of your order. Make sure you also keep the name and address of the company with which you are dealing.

6. Do not rely solely on the picture. Note the description, size, weight, color, and contents. Be sure to include this along with the order number.

7. Make sure you give the company complete information. Be very explicit. Make sure you include all information about your order.

8. Be sure to enclose shipping, handling, and tax charges with your order.

9. To get *on* a mailing list or to get *off* the mailing list write to Direct Mail Marketing Association, Mail Preference Service, 6 East 43rd Street, New York, N.Y. 10017.

10. If you feel you were cheated, be sure to let the post office know, because it may fall under the mail fraud law.

Mail-Order Houses

There is no limit to what you can purchase by mail order. Here is a sampling of solutions offering a wide variety of products and a wider range of prices.

1. Annie's Attic, Rte. 2, Box 212 B, Big Sandy, Tex. 75755—Patterns for making needlework articles.
2. Boston Museum Shop, Museum of Fine Arts, P.O. Box 1044, Boston, Mass. 02120—Beautifully crafted items for your own home or for gifts.
3. Bruce Bolind, 8 Bolind Building, Boulder, Colo. 80302—Gift items, household items. Catalog costs $1.
4. Burpee Seed Co., 24-310 Burpee Building, Warminster, Penn. 18974; or 17-32 Burpee Building, Clinton, Iowa 52732; or P.O. Box 748, Riverside, Calif. 92502—Send for catalog from address nearest you.
5. Century Family Products, 3628 Crenshaw Boulevard, Los Angeles, Calif. 90016—Home entertainment accessories. Record and cassette cases and files, photograph albums, magazine binders, photograph frames, scrap books.
6. Colonial Garden Kitchen, 270 West Merrick Road, Valley Stream, N.Y. 11582—Items for the home.
7. Country Curtains, Department 102, Stockbridge, Mass. 01262—Old fashioned country house curtains in assorted fabrics and styles. Wide range of sizes. Also bedspreads, tablecloths, etc.
8. Ferry House, Department W 923, Briarcliff Manor, N.Y. 10510—Clothing, household and gift items.
9. Fran's Basket House, Route 10, Succasunna, N.J. 07876—Baskets of various sizes, rattan magazine racks, wall holders for mail, receipts, etc.
10. Frostline Kits, 452 Burbank Street, Broomfield, Colo. 80020—Kits for making sleeping bags, comforters, parkas, raingear, tents, backpacks, and bike packs.
11. Harriet Carter, Department 14109, Plymouth Meeting, Penn. 19462—Gifts, novelties, household items. Pet books and supplies, personal and beauty items. Kitchen and bathroom items, stationery, Christmas decorations and ornaments, games and sports books.
12. Helen Gallagher, Department F 545, Peoria, Ill. 61601—Decorative accessories for every room of the house. Imports as well as American favorites.
13. Just for Kids, Winterbrook Way, Meredith, N.H. 03253
14. L.L. Bean, Inc., 141 Cedar Street, Freeport, Maine 04033—Camping and sports equipment. Sportswear and footwear for men and women.
15. Lane Bryant, Department A, Indianapolis, Ind. 46201—Large-size and half-size clothes for women.
16. LeeWard's American Home Craft Centers, 1200 St. Charles Road, Elgin, Ill. 60120—Crafts and needlework needs.

17. Lillian Vernon, 510 South Fulton Avenue, Mt. Vernon, N.Y. 10550—An innovative collection of gifts, many personalized.
18. Lilies, Box 774-E, Port Townsend, Wash. 98368—Hundreds of world-famous garden varieties of lilies.
19. Metropolitan Museum of Art, Box 255 Gracie Station, New York, N.Y. 10161—Exact copies of ancient jewelry, early American glass and pewter, and needlepoint adaptions. Cards and notes. Special catalog of gifts for children.
20. Miles Kimball, 41 West 8th Avenue, Oshkosh, Wis. 54901—Household items and gifts, children's toys, workshop, automobile, sports, and pet supplies. They also offer some items of special interest to the handicapped, such as sheet and blanket supports, thermal pads, and fire escape ladders.
21. Outdoor Gallery, Box 308, Point Roberts, Wash. 98281—Full-color prints of your favorite breed of dog. Decorative items pertaining to pets, for example, colorful keyrings featuring your favorite breed of cat.
22. George W. Park Seed Company, 180 Cokesbury Road, Greenwood, S.C. 29647—Their full-color catalog lists a full selection of bulbs, perennials, house plants, gardening accessories, and gifts.
23. Pepperidge Farms, Mail-Order Company, Inc., P.O. Box 119, Route 145, Clinton, Conn. 06413—Food products.
24. Shopping International, Department 404, Norwich, Vt. 05055—Fine fashions, jewelry, and handcrafts. Catalog available for $1.
25. Spencer Gifts, Inc., Mail-Order Division, Atlantic City, N.J. 08411—Gifts, novelties, plus items for the handicapped, such as contour pillow, hygienic pants, safety bathtub rails, knee warmers, and other items.
26. Starcrest of California, 3159 Red Hill Avenue, Costa Mesa, Calif. 92626—Self-hypnosis tapes, needlepoint sets, clothing, household items, gifts, cozy cuff warmers, paint keeper palette, etc.
27. The Left Hand, 140 West 22nd Street, New York, N.Y. 10011—Over 100 products especially designed for the "southpaw"—from playing cards to a left-hand can opener. Catalog available for $1.
28. The Swiss Colony, 1112 7th Avenue, Monroe, Wis. 53566—Cheese, sausages, etc.
29. Walter Drake, 3059 Drake Building, Colorado Springs, Colo. 80940—Personalized stationery, pet supplies, and household supplies.
30. Yield House, Box 1000, North Conway, N.H. 02860—Furniture, decorative household items, and gifts.

And, of course, you don't want to overlook the old reliables, such as Sears Roebuck and Company, Montgomery Ward, or Spiegel catalogs. Also the advertising sections in the back of magazines list many more mail-order suppliers from which to choose.

A Few Random Suggestions for Saving Money

1. Patronizing a beauty school or barber college instead of a regular beauty salon or barber shop can save up to fifty percent or more of what you would otherwise pay.

2. Thrift shops are available in almost every area that feature clothing, home furnishings, books, dishes and many other items.

3. Factory outlets and discount stores can offer some excellent bargains if you know your merchandise and choose carefully.

4. Trading products or services either on a one-to-one basis or as part of a group can save considerable sums. For example, one woman bakes cakes and makes fancy desserts, which she trades for some sewing or mending she's unable to do. One man who is in a wheelchair does beautiful printing and sign making, which he exchanges for someone to paint a room in his house or whatever. Look for things you are able to do or make that someone else cannot. Decide ahead on how much money or time is involved to work out a fair exchange.

5. Consult some of the many books or booklets available on getting the most for your shopping dollar in food, clothing, and household goods, so you can get the most for dollars spent.

6. For the fifty-five or older group, there are organizations such as the American Association of Retired People that offer drugs and vitamins at reduced costs through the mail.

7. Many theaters have reduced rates for afternoon matinees that are considerably less expensive than evening rates.

8. Newspapers often have coupons for restaurants that offer two dinners for the price of one. Or take-out, fast-food places may offer two pizzas or hamburgers for the price of one, or they may offer special family/group discounts.

9. Almost everyone who has a garden or raises indoor plants is happy to give away a cutting or slip of a plant. If they are separating bulbs, etc., they often have extras to spare.

10. If you want to eat out at a good restaurant, make it for lunch instead of dinner. You'll get the same fine food at a lower price.

11. If you need minor plumbing, electrical, or household repairs done, call one of the retirement job centers or a handyman. This is much less expensive than a regular full-time plumber or electrician.

12. You may want to join a refunding club or subscribe to one of the refunding newsletters. Getting into coupon saving and exchanging is fun, and it really stretches your supermarket dollars.

chapter eleven
THOSE FAR AWAY PLACES

It is no longer an impossible dream to reach those far away places with the strange sounding names. Today your destination need only be limited by your dreams and by your pocketbook, not by your disability.

Anyone ready to venture forth for the first time will thank those who have pioneered the way and shared their experiences. The information they've gathered is exciting and useful whether for planning a long trip or a short one. Using the knowledge and experiences of other handicapped travelers will make traveling easier regardless of whether you are using a cane, crutches, or a wheelchair.

Travel Agencies—How They Can Help

1. Ability Tours, Inc., 729 Delaware Avenue SW, Washington, D.C. 20024
2. Anchor Travel Agency, 1631 Garnet, San Diego, Calif. 92101—Authorized agents for airline tickets, tours, cruises, hotels, and car rentals. They specialize in providing accessible facilities.

3. C.I. Mobility Services, Division of Cruise International, 250 Janaf Plaza, Norfolk, Va. 23502—Offers complete travel services for the handicapped with individual trip planning and research and special escorted tour packages to several countries. They provide volunteer travel aides.
4. Evergreen Travel Service, 19505L 44th Avenue West, Lynnwood, Wa. 98036—This agency has been operating tours for the handicapped for many years. They offer services for disabilities including tours for the blind. They list tours to Europe, Hawaii, Indonesia, Alaska, and the Carribbean.
5. Flying Wheels Tours, P.O. Box 382, 143 West Bridge Street, Owatonna, Minn. 55060—The owner, Judd Jacobson, is a quadriplegic from a swimming accident. He owns two travel agencies in Minnesota that provide tours for the physically handicapped, their relatives, and their friends. The tours provide for even the most severely disabled.

    Lifting and transfers into airplanes and limousines are included, as well as meeting routine needs, such as emptying urinal bags, help in and out of bed, etc. Extra care, such as dressing, involved nursing, and feeding can be arranged for an agreed-upon price. If you need a companion, Flying Wheels has a list of well-qualified people who are willing to travel as attendant/companions. This agency lists tours to Las Vegas, Grand Canyon, and other places in the United States, trips by plane to Hawaii, Europe, and the Orient, as well as a Carribbean cruise.
6. Getz International Travel Agency, 640 Sacramento Street, San Francisco, Calif. 94119
7. Handy-Cap Horizons, 3250 East Loretta Drive, Indianapolis, Ind. 47227—This is a nonprofit organization that has been operating trips since 1963 and specializes in people-to-people contacts in other countries. European tours and a Carribbean cruise are among their offerings.
8. Kerr Travel Agency, 9301 Wilshire Boulevard, Beverly Hills, Calif. 90210—The owner, Mrs. Alathena Miller, is in a wheelchair because of polio. She has traveled widely and will be glad to offer suggestions and advice. Contact her for further information.
9. Pinetree Tours, Inc., 3600 Wilshire Boulevard, Suite 1516, Los Angeles, Calif. 90010
10. Rambling Tours, Inc., P.O. Box 1304, Hallandale, Fla. 33009—Ruth and Murray Fein also offer complete travel services to the physically disabled, their families, and their friends. In addition to European tours, this agency lists tours to Central America, including Guatemala, Costa Rica, and the Republic of Panama. One of their tours includes North Africa.

OTHER TRAVEL AGENCIES

Your phone book may contain the names of travel agencies in your area that plan trips for handicapped travelers, or a local travel agent may suggest one.

Special Preparations

Last minute trip preparations can evoke a shudder in the hardiest traveler, so why not organize and pace yourself so you avoid those last minute hassles?

Travelers with any sort of condition limiting their mobility or endurance should consider using a wheelchair when traveling. You don't want to be so tired or in so much pain that you can't enjoy your trip, so plan ahead.

If you are in a wheelchair, have it checked before you leave. Do take the manufacturer's instruction booklet along in case you need any kind of service or repair in another country where they may not be familiar with American-made wheelchairs. And do pack a small repair kit so you can take care of any minor problems.

Be sure to carry extra cane or crutch tips, so you won't be caught with a lost or damaged one you can't easily replace. If you use a cane, consider purchasing a folding model for convenience while traveling. If you travel with any equipment run by electricity, be sure to provide ahead of time for any necessary adaptation device you might need.

It's a good idea to etch your identification on your equipment or have it labeled in some way that can't be easily removed.

One traveler suggests taking along a bicycle lock for your wheelchair for those times you transfer and leave your chair parked.

Tips for Packing

Folding clothes is difficult for those of you with uncooperative fingers, so try rolling them instead next time. Your garments will be easier to manipulate, and they will emerge with fewer wrinkles.

Shawls and stoles are easier to pack than sweaters and are not so bulky to carry, put on, or take off.

Always pack a sun hat for those waits in sunny places where there are no shelters.

Pack all liquids, cosmetics, and medicines securely in aluminum foil or plastic Ziploc bags. Otherwise you may have a sticky mess in your suitcase.

One traveler says she always carries an infant nursing bottle filled with water in her purse or tote bag for those times she may need to take a pill when there's no water handy.

And don't forget to include a box of premoistened towelettes, always keeping a few in your purse or pocket when you need to wash your hands and there's no washroom available.

For those of you on crutches, a good backpack is indispensable. Be sure you get one that hangs comfortably. When buying one for a wheelchair, be sure that it doesn't impede wheel rotation.

And for anyone who will be trying to manage their own luggage, buy a set of detachable wheels if your luggage doesn't have built-in ones.

Medical Preparations for Your Trip

If you are on any medication that you must take regularly, always carry some with you in your purse, small carry-on bag, or other safe place. You may be separated from your luggage for a longer time than planned or, heaven forbid, it may get misplaced or lost. It is a good idea to take an extra prescription with you to cover unexpected delays, losses, or other emergencies. Be sure the prescription lists the generic name of the drug you are taking, as this may be of great importance in a foreign country as well as in your own.

One woman planned a two-week camping trip in a remote part of northern Idaho. On a stop enroute, her purse containing her prescription medicine was stolen. It took three days to get another prescription and then there was difficulty having it filled because the local pharmacy didn't carry the drug. The incident spoiled her vacation. In some cases such a loss would be disastrous.

It is also wise to carry an extra pair of eyeglasses or contact lenses with you if being without them would incapacitate you.

Medical Help When Traveling

There are three associations which can be of special value to the handicapped traveler. The International Association for Medical Assistance for Travelers (IAMAT) is a group of physicians who speak various languages. For example, if you became ill while traveling in France, you could contact a doctor who speaks English and communicate your problem to him. Anyone can belong to this association without a fee or for a small donation. When you join you receive a brochure listing doctors in various countries.

Similar medical assistance is provided by Intermedic, which has a directory of about 300 English-speaking physicians in 170 cities in eighty-nine countries. The directory has space for the member's photograph and personal medical history.

For persons with hidden medical conditions, such as diabetes, heart ailments, and allergies, the Medic Alert Foundation in Turlock, California, will provide a tag, bracelet, or necklace inscribed with the bearer's file number, his or her medical problem, and a hot-line telephone number. In the event of an emergency, the number in California can be called collect from anywhere in the world twenty-four hours a day for detailed information on the patient from the Foundation's central files.

Further information on the three organizations mentioned above can be obtained by writing to the following addresses.

1. IAMAT, 350 5th Avenue, New York, N.Y. 10001
2. Intermedic, 777 3rd Avenue, New York, N.Y. 10017
3. Medic Alert Foundation, P.O. Box 10009, Turlock, Calif. 95380

Good Health in Four Languages

Travelers bound for Europe or Latin America no longer need to worry about the language problem if illness or accident strikes them. Blue Cross Association has published A FOREIGN LANGUAGE GUIDE TO HEALTH CARE. Thic pocketsize booklet is filled with phrases covering almost every medical and emergency situation in French, German, Italian, and Spanish, along with phonetic pronunciation guides. The booklet also contains useful tips on immunization, locating doctors in a foreign country, and getting reimbursed by the health insurance that covers your trip. You can get a free copy from any Blue Cross office in the United States.

When You Plan to Fly

Each U.S. airline is now required to have a national company policy regarding handicapped travelers that has been approved by the Federal Aviation Agency, but these policies vary from airline to airline. A survey of the airlines reveals a wide difference in policies, ranging from accepting all passengers with no restrictions to only accepting a wheelchair passenger for flights of three hours or less.

Many airlines provide assistance during boarding and deplaning procedures to anyone weighing 175 pounds or less. If you weigh more you may be asked to provide your own assistant both at the point of origin and destination.

Some airlines require the handicapped passenger to have an attendant, and most airplanes say they cannot provide someone to help a handicapped person to the restroom or someone to feed a handicapped person.

You should plan ahead by contacting the airline you plan to fly with, so you will know what help they can give and what rules or regulations they have pertaining to handicapped passengers.

Describe the disability and make sure the airline will accept you as a passenger and provide any assistance needed. They will need to know the following information:

1. Are you in a wheelchair or do you only need one at the airport?
2. Can you walk on level ground but need help with steps?
3. Will you need help in getting to the bathroom?
4. Do you have any other special needs or limitations?
5. If you have a motorized wheelchair, be sure to tell them what kind of batteries it uses, as some types will not be allowed on board unless packed separately.

Ask any questions and make any special requests at this time. Reservation clerks should be able to advise which flights are less crowded and which ones are direct, so you can avoid unnecessary plane changes.

Allow yourself plenty of time and arrive early enough so you can be boarded ahead of other passengers if the airline suggests this.

Blind persons who are not officially classified as handicapped by most airlines, may request guides and early boarding in order to orient themselves to the plane. Generally, seeing-eye dogs travel free in the cabin with their owners. But it is vital to check this in advance with the airline and the air terminals you will be using. Not all airports allow these animals even to enter passenger areas.

Deaf persons who anticipate any difficulties should make inquiries in advance. Cabin attendants on the flight should be notified that a deaf person is on board. Cabin attendants can then draw the deaf person's attention to cards outlining emergency procedures and safety regulations and to "no smoking" and "fasten seat belt" signs. Announcements made on the intercom systems during flight, such as turbulence being encountered or anticipated flight delays, could be communicated to deaf passengers in writing.

Airlines and airports are beginning to extend the same privileges to hearing-ear dogs as they do to seeing-eye dogs. Recently the FAA requested all airports serving scheduled airlines to install amplified telephones for the deaf.

As is the case with many new company policies, the word doesn't always sift down to all personnel. If you do not receive a satisfactory answer from a reservations clerk, you may contact an official of the airline. If you wish to have the regulations regarding your handicap in writing, you may request that these be sent to you.

More and more airports are becoming accessible to the handicapped. If you use a wheelchair and fly in or out of Los Angeles International Air Terminal, you can park in special reserved wheelchair parking spaces, and lift-equipped vans will take you to your airline terminal. For more information write for:

GUIDE FOR THE HANDICAPPED AND ELDERLY
Los Angeles International Airport, Public Relations Bureau, Los

Angeles Department of Airports, 1 World Way, Los Angeles, Calif. 90009.

Handicapped airline passengers passing through Chicago's O'Hare International Airport will find a unique brochure at the information booth of each domestic terminal. It has a map and detailed description of special facilities available. To obtain the brochure write for:

AIRPORT GUIDE FOR THE HANDICAPPED AND ELDERLY
Chicago O'Hare International Airport, Chicago Department of Aviation, City Hall, Room 1111, Chicago, Ill. 60602.

At San Francisco airport they have a Handicapped Travelers Association, which provides, among other things, assistance for check-in and check-out, deplaning and boarding, and more detailed information. It also has battery rental and recharging services for those who use electric wheelchairs. It has the TTY PortaPrinter II equipment and does signing and interpreting for the deaf. There is an operations and information booth in the main lobby.

For information on other airports, write to any of the following:

FACILITIES AND SERVICES FOR THE HANDICAPPED: NEWARK INTERNATIONAL, LAGUARDIA, AND KENNEDY INTERNATIONAL AIRPORTS
Port Authority of New York and New Jersey, Aviation Public Service Division, 1 World Trade Center, Room 65N, New York, N.Y. 10048

GUIDE FOR THE HANDICAPPED
Dallas–Fort Worth Airport, Easter Seal Society of Texas, Inc., 4429 N. Central Expressway, Dallas, Tex. 75205

AIR TRAVEL FOR THE HANDICAPPED
Trans World Airlines, Inc.—Available at any of the local offices.

CARE IN THE AIR: ADVICE FOR HANDICAPPED PASSENGERS
Air Transport Users Committee, 129 Kingsway, London, England WC2B 6NN

FLIGHT INFORMATION FOR BLIND PASSENGERS, and
FLIGHT INFORMATION FOR THE PHYSICALLY HANDICAPPED
Frontier Airlines, 8250 Smith Road, Denver, Colo. 30207—The pamphlet for blind passengers is available in Braille.

CARRIAGE OF THE PHYSICALLY HANDICAPPED ON DOMESTIC AND INTERNATIONAL AIRLINES
United Cerebral Palsy Association, Inc., 66 East 34th Street, New York, N.Y. 10016—Pamphlet available for a nominal fee.

ACCESS TRAVEL: AIRPORTS—A GUIDE TO ACCESSIBILITY OF TERMINALS
Airport Operators Council International, 1700 K Street NW, Washington, D.C. 20006

TRAVEL FOR THE HANDICAPPED
United Airlines, Consumer Affairs Department, P.O. Box 66100, Chicago, Ill. 60666

CHARTER AIRLINES
Many charter airlines can accommodate a handicapped traveler. Some small planes can remove seats to accommodate a wheelchair or stretcher. This can be an expensive way to travel, but there may be times when it would be an advantage or a real necessity.

HOT LINE FOR AIRLINE TRAVELERS
If you are refused passage on a commercial airline flight or if you have problems with any airline personnnel, you can call a hot line set up by the Civil Aeronautics Board in Washington, D.C. The hot line is open twenty-four hours a day. The number is (202) 382-7735. Those wanting to send written complaints can write to the Director of Consumer Affairs, Civil Aeronautics Board, 1875 Constitution Avenue, Washington, D.C. 20428.

Car Rentals

Rental cars with hand controls are now available in a number of cities; however, advance planning is essential. The policies vary from one company to another, so it pays to shop around. Some car rental agencies do not charge extra for hand-drive controls, and some ask for an extra deposit. Many times you will have to deal with supervisory personnel rather than one of the clerks who may not know how to handle your problem. It is wise to call at least two weeks ahead and make your reservations through the national toll-free number listed in the yellow pages of most telephone books.

When You Go by Train

Train travel is still a problem for many disabled travelers. Amtrak has some cars with special facilities for the handicapped. However, they will not solve the problem of stations and trains with steps impossible for a passenger in a wheelchair to mount without assistance.

New AMfleet cars, which will be used on short- or moderate-length runs, have a special seat in the dining car. They also have an accessible bathroom if wheelchairs will go through a door thirty inches wide. Turboliners, for longer runs, have sleeping cars with at least one accessible compartment. Because of the limited number of these special facilities, those who wish to make use of them should book well in advance.

You should have someone evaluate the facilities to see if your particular disability can be accommodated. Company officials say roomettes or bedrooms are a possibility if there is an attendant or companion along. The restrooms, however, do not accommodate wheelchairs. If you only need a wheelchair from depot to the train and can use the train restrooms without assistance, you can easily manage.

Amtrak offers handicapped travelers and senior citizens a twenty-five percent discount on any train when the regular one-way fare is $40 or more. To receive the discount, disabled persons need to present either a card from a state or local government or from a service organization or a letter from a doctor. There are no longer discounts for attendants traveling with disabled persons. Amtrak requests reservations be made at least a month in advance.

Amtrak has a teletypewriter (TTY)—a telephone one types on rather than talks into—for use by the deaf. The user types a message or question into the machine (similar to a typewriter). The machine transmits electronic impulses via the telephone to teletype equipment at Amtrak's office in Philadelphia. Amtrak operators type answering messages into their machines, which are in turn received on the caller's TTY.

Amtrak has a brochure for handicapped travelers entitled *Access Amtrak*. To request copies, write to Amtrak Public Affairs, 955 L'Enfant Plaza SW, Washington, D.C. 20024.

Travel by Bus

Travel by bus is still difficult for most handicapped individuals, but the situation is changing for the better. Greyhound's Helping Hand Program and Trailway's Good Samaritan Program encourage handicapped persons to take a bus with a companion.

With a doctor's certificate that assistance is needed, you can have a companion travel with you *at no extra charge.* Your wheelchair, crutches, walker, or similar device is carried in the baggage compartment without charge and does not count as part of your allowable luggage.

However, the aisles on the buses are only fourteen inches wide, which may make them impossible to negotiate. Bus terminal restrooms are still a problem in many areas, as are eating facilities, which are not always inside of or close to the bus depot. As bus depots are remodeled or new ones built, the needs of the handicapped are being met.

To find out if you can use restaurants and restrooms at stations along the way, Greyhound advises you to request the ticket agent to secure this information from headquarters several days before departure. This may help in choosing between alternate routes.

Food is available at rest stops and Greyhound terminals. However, you may wish to bring along a sandwich, fruit, or snacks to tide you over between hot meals.

A small carry-on handbag or duffel bag is a good idea, especially if you require scheduled or emergency medication. The bag may be stowed in the rack above your seat and be ready when you need it.

One more thing to consider: You may have to change buses on some schedules or, if traveling on a connecting bus, you may have to transfer to a different terminal. Be sure to check this out thoroughly when you first inquire about schedule information. This way you can plan your trip most conveniently.

Blind persons can travel at discounted rates on Greyhound, and both national bus lines allow seeing-eye and hearing-ear dogs to accompany their owners. Write to this address for more information on the Helping Hand Program, or inquire at your local bus station: Director of Customer Relations, Greyhound Lines, Greyhound Tower, Phoenix, Ariz. 85077.

Write to this address for information on the Good Samaritan Program, or inquire at your local bus station: Continental Trailways, 1512 Commerce Street, Dallas, Tex. 75201.

Travel by Car, Camper, Van, or Motor Home

For those who want to travel extensively without the hassle of worrying about accessible restrooms and restaurants or of boarding buses, trains, or planes, there are many options that may offer the freedom you desire. The choices range from regular automobiles with hand controls or other adaptations to vans with wheelchair lifts and campers or trailers modified to individual needs, or to Winnebago motor homes large enough to accommodate a rocking bed for a post-polio traveler.

One couple looking for a motor home to accommodate the wife's wheelchair settled on a twenty-one-foot Winnebago. The swivel passenger chair allowed her to ride in comfort. By removing one of the dinette seats, there was more room for her wheelchair. The motor home provided running water, a gas stove, an oven, a refrigerator, and a bathroom with toilet, sink, and shower.

If your vehicle is not self-contained and you are considering a camping trip, you will have to check out accessible campgrounds by writing or phoning ahead. For those of you who are interested in enjoying the fun, activities, and fellowship of other recreational vehicle owners, there are many travel clubs available.

The American Automobile Association (AAA) has a directory listing and describing more than 500 transportation services for handicapped drivers, including driving schools and manufacturers of handicapped driving aids. It gives names, addresses, and phone numbers for these services. Copies of the directory can be obtained from the nearest AAA office by asking for THE HANDICAPPED DRIVER'S MOBILITY GUIDE. It is available for a small fee.

A directory of highway rest stops geared to the handicapped traveler is available free from the Federal Highway Administration, U.S. Department of Transportation, Washington, D.C. 20590.

Hotel/Motel Guides

1. BEST WESTERN TRAVEL GUIDE
   2910 Sky Harbor Boulevard, Phoenix, Ariz. 85034—This free guide indicates some 300 accessible properties, primarily in North America.

2. HOLIDAY INN DIRECTORY
   Holiday Inns, Inc., Public Relations Hotel Group, 3796 Lamar Avenue, Memphis, Tenn. 38118—This free accommodations guide indicates some 625 accessible properties. They have a TTY (teletypewriter) that enables the deaf to make reservations at all of their hotels and motels. The toll-free number is (800) 238-5544.

3. HOWARD JOHNSON DIRECTORY
   222 Forbes Road, Braintree, Mass. 02184—Free directory indicates some 300 accessible properties.

4. MARRIOTT HOTELS DIRECTORY
   Marriott Corporation, Marriott Drive, Washington, D. C. 20058—Marriott's directory indicates all properties that are accessible. Free upon request.

5. QUALITY INNS DIRECTORY
   Marketing Department, 10750 Columbia Pike, Silver Spring, Md. 20901—Free coded directory indicates some 100 accessible properties.

6. RAMADA INNS DIRECTORY
   Ramada Inns, Inc., P.O. Box 590, Phoenix, Ariz. 85001—Free directory indicates some 455 accessible properties.

7. RODEWAY INNS DIRECTORY
   Rodeway Inns of America, 2525 Stemmons Freeway, Suite 800, Dallas, Tex. 75207—Free directory indicating accessible properties.

8. WESTERN INTERNATIONAL HOTEL FACILITIES FOR THE HANDICAPPED
   Western International Hotels, 2000 5th Avenue, Seattle, Wash. 98121—Free directory includes domestic and foreign properties that are accessible.

9. DOWNTOWNER/ROWNTOWNER INNS
   Directory of Inns, Hotel Systems of America, Box 171807, Memphis, Tenn. 38117—For information call their toll-free number—(800) 238-6161.

10. HANDICABS OF THE PACIFIC
    P.O. Box 22428, Honolulu, Hawaii 96822—They offer wheelchair taxi service for transfer to and from the airports, sightseeing tours, nightclubbing, and shopping. Write them for further information. Booklet is free.

Travel Books and Pamphlets

THE WHEELCHAIR TRAVELER, Douglass R. Annand
Ball Hill Road, Milford, N.H. 03055—Mr. Annand is a paraplegic who has been in a wheelchair for the past twenty-one years. He has traveled extensively, gathering and up-dating material for his book. It lists hotels, motels, restaurants, and sightseeing attractions that are accessible to the handicapped traveler. It provides much information, such as width of door openings, if there are any steps, and other special information. It contains a rating system that will help you judge just how useful the listing would be for you. No listing is guaranteed, but all are from knowledgeable sources. Small fee.

WHEELCHAIR AIR TRAVEL, Clare Miller
Box 7, Blair, Cambridge, Ontario, Canada—The book was written by a paraplegic who operates a small travel business in Canada. This small booklet not only offers tips on travel but also tells the author's unusual and humorous experiences in other countries. Small charge.

TRAVELABILITY: A GUIDE FOR PHYSICALLY DISABLED TRAVELERS IN THE UNITED STATES, Lois Reamy
Macmillan, New York, N.Y. 10022—A step-by-step guide to safe, carefree trip planning for the physically disabled. It includes information on various modes of transportation, medical matters, and tips on hotels and motels with barrier-free rooms. Small charge.

ACCESS TO THE WORLD, Louise Weiss
Chatham Square Press, New York, N.Y.—Small charge.

TRAVEL TIPS FOR THE HANDICAPPED
Consumer Information Center, Pueblo, Colo. 81009—Information on air travel, train travel, bus travel, and rental cars. Free.

ACCESS TRAVEL: AIRPORTS
Consumer Information Center, Pueblo, Colo. 81009—Information on facilities at domestic and foreign airports from Aberdeen, Scotland, to Zurich, Switzerland. It includes parking facilities, walkways, public areas in buildings, airplane boarding areas, airport restrooms, and telephones. It also includes information on rental of hand-controlled cars. Free.

GUIDEBOOKS FOR HANDICAPPED TRAVELERS
President's Committee on Employment of the Handicapped, 1111 20th and L Streets NW, Washington, D.C. 20210—Free.

A LIST OF GUIDEBOOKS FOR HANDICAPPED TRAVELERS
National Center for a Barrier-Free Environment, 8401 Connecticut Avenue NW, Washington, D.C. 20015—Tells how to obtain guidebooks for over ninety American cities and states and twenty-six foreign cities and countries describing the hotels, museums, restaurants, department stores, churches, and other attractions that accommodate handicapped tourists. Free.

TRAVEL FOR THE PATIENT WITH CHRONIC OBSTRUCTIVE PULMONARY DISEASES
Rehabilitation Research Training Center, George Washington University Medical Center, Ross Hall, Room 714, 2300 Eye Street NW, Washington, D.C. 20037—Free.

NATIONAL PARK GUIDE FOR THE HANDICAPPED
Superintendent of Documents, U.S. Government Printing Office, Washington, D.C. 20402—Free.

ACCESS—NATIONAL PARKS
Consumer Information Center, Department 102F, Pueblo, Colo. 81009—The guide lists accessible features of more than 300 park areas. Available for a small fee.

ACCESS NEW YORK
Access New York, Publications Department, Institute of Rehabilitative Medicine, 400 North 34th Street, New York, N.Y. 10016—Lists more than 750 midtown restaurants, hotels, theaters, stores, government buildings, houses of worship, libraries, and community centers that are easily accessible to disabled individuals. Available for a small fee.

ORLANDO'S GUIDE FOR THE HANDICAPPED
Orlando Tourist Trade Association, P.O. Box 15492, Orlando, Fla. 32858—Guide includes a representative list of hotels, restaurants, shopping centers, and other public places and gives information on their accessibility. It also provides information about amusement centers, including Disney World and Sea World, and hospitals, libraries, and the availability of medical services in the area. Free.

INTERNATIONAL DIRECTORY OF ACCESS GUIDES
Rehabilitation International, USA, 20 West 40th Street, New York, N.Y. 10018—*No* charge for this guide for disabled and elderly travelers. It is compiled by the staff of Rehabilitation World. It includes many U.S. cities, as well as some in Europe, Australia, Bermuda, and Canada. They also offer a free listing of travel agencies or tour operators that serve the disabled.

Moss Rehabilitation Travel Center, 12th Street and Tabor Road, Philadelphia, Penn. 19141—The Moss Rehabilitation Hospital of Philadelphia devoted two years gathering information about travel accommodations. You can learn which hotels and motels have ramps, which airlines make an extra effort to accommodate the disabled, and which historical sites, tourist attractions, and national monuments are accessible to the handicapped. In writing for information, outline which cities or countries you want to visit and what your special interests are. The Center will send you all the available information they have on the site or country you wish to visit.

ROLLIN' ON—A WHEELCHAIR GUIDE TO U.S. CITIES, Maxine Atwater
Dodd, Mead, 79 Madison Avenue, New York, N.Y. 10016—

Provides information about trip planning to and within eight popular U.S. cities and appropriate accommodations in each city. Contains information on over fifty daily and mini tours and suggestions on places of interest and the best way to see them. Designed to be used as both a travel planner and guide at each destination.

Gadgets for Gadabouts

A small brochure, TRAVELER'S CHECKLIST, offers several items most helpful for handicapped travelers. It is available from Traveler's Checklist, Cornwall Bridge Road, Sharon, Conn. 06069. Here is a random sampling of the items listed and their descriptions.

A. Travel organizer—Beautifully compact design to carry all your toiletries in a minimum of space. Just unfold and hang up on handy ring. Three zippered compartments hold everything from hairspray cans to jewelry and more. Case folds up and secures with spring clasp. Soft leather-like vinyl. Open, measures 12 by 10 inches; closed—6½ by 10 inches. Black or bone.

B. Pocket valise—A full-size spare valise, folds into a matching envelope that slips into your pocket or purse for the special things you buy en route.

C. Universal travel adapter—Device contains four different plugs (American, Continental, British, and scarce Australian) in one compact unit. Plus Edison screw and pin sockets, all in self-contained case.

D. Expand-a-Bag—Slip it over your shoulder to carry your wallet, passport, etc. Also unzips into a full-size travel bag. Made of sturdy nylon faille, has detachable shoulder strap and carry handles. Closed, measures 6½ by 5 by 3 inches; open—20½ by 12¾ by 5½ inches. Red, blue, brown, or black.

E. The Helping Handle—An extra hand for juggling luggage, etc. Loops around handle and snaps closed in seconds. Lets you carry two things in one hand. Stows easily and neatly in case or purse. Brown or black.

F. Therma-Pak cordless heating pad—Cordless, so it can be used anywhere, anytime. Six-inch-square heating pad actually molds itself to your body. Needs only two tablespoons of water to give you the soothing moist heat you want for hours. Ideal for travel, home, etc. Complete with travel case.

G. Deluxe Kart-a-Bag—Totes up to one hundred pounds; weighs only four pounds. Entire unit folds down to 20 inches long, tucks into handsome simulated leather case.

H. Luggage caddy—Like having your own porter. The heavy-duty straps attach to suitcase in seconds. Detachable wheels tuck into own tote. Lightweight—two pounds.

I. Mini-laundry—Time and money saver. Contains elastic twist clothesline, four unbreakable clothes clips, detergent, all in handy case.

J. Rechargeable pocket flashlight—Handy for reading maps at night and during occasional power failures. No batteries. Can be recharged by plugging it into ordinary wall socket. Has twin bulbs for white or red beam. Fits into pocket or purse.

Now that you know it is possible to visit many exciting places with the assistance of knowledgeable travel agencies, cooperative airlines, and helpful books to guide you, perhaps you can make those dreams come true.

chapter twelve
YOU CAN RIDE A HOBBY HORSE

A hobby can be any pastime one chooses to pursue for enjoyment. If you find yourself with more spare time than you wish because you are recuperating from a broken arm or leg, are laid up in a cast, or have a long-term disability, why not consider a new hobby? Or, if you already have one, it might be fun to choose another one to perk up your spirits and add variety to life.

Reading or Listening to Books

Reading can take you any place in the world, offer adventure, suspense, mystery, or romance. It can take you back to any period in history you choose and introduce you to brilliant minds in science or any field you choose. It can also cover the current scene for you. Your choices are endless.

In addition to the regular books you may borrow from your local library, many libraries have talking books and will lend them to anyone who needs them. They also lend the record player or tape recorder for records or cassettes.

Some communities have bookmobiles that take books to various sections of large cities or outlying areas. Others have Special Outreach Services which bring books, magazines, paperbacks, large print books, records, cassette tapes, talking books, art prints, and paintings to your home free of charge.

Your local library can also obtain talking books from the Library of Congress for you. There is a free talking book catalog available from the Library of Congress, Washington, D.C. 20540. They also supply remote control units, earphones, and other special equipment to meet a variety of needs. To be eligible you need a statement from a doctor, nurse, or any qualified person stating your disability.

READER'S DIGEST, GUIDEPOSTS, and many other magazines and books are available in large print. Your library can tell you where to obtain them.

Collecting

Collecting can be fun. Your choice can be anything from bells and buttons to sea shells and spoons. Your choice may depend not only on interest but on how much space you have and how much money you can afford to spend.

Stamp collecting does not cost a lot to get started, and you can add as much or as little as you wish. Friends can save you their stamps from faraway places and you can trade them.

Coin collecting is another popular choice that friends can help you with. One collector with cerebral palsy uses a small portable automatic coin packing machine, since he cannot use his hands to repack stacks of coins after sorting.

You may think there is nothing terribly interesting about collecting matchbooks, but when they are categorized and lovingly displayed they become stimulating and exciting. Each one has its own story or brings back a special memory. "This one we got at Yosemite the summer we got lost on a hike and had to spend an unexpected night on the trail."

One man whose hobby is collecting old guns says one of the good things that evolved as a result of his hobby is the growing number of guys who became close friends because of a common interest. Even though largely housebound, friends drop by to show him their latest find, talk guns, history, or what have you.

Whether you collect miniatures, cups and saucers, or model airplanes, the important thing is that it holds your interest. If you try collecting coins or stamps and find it just doesn't satisfy you, don't hesitate to drop it and try the next thing that sounds interesting. If collecting just isn't for you, don't hesitate to switch to something entirely different.

Don't say "I can't afford it," because there are lots of things you can collect that cost little or no money. There are so many things like leaves, shells, rock specimens, matchbooks, postcards, etc. The list is limited only by your imagination.

Music

Music can be enjoyed via radio, TV, records, and cassettes. Your friends may bring over a stack of their favorites to share with you, or you can borrow records and cassettes from your local library.

Don't rule out the possibility of making your own music. A harmonica, with a few hours of practice, can provide a lot of enjoyment. When you become really good, you might want to join a harmonica club or start one of your own.

If you have use of your hands, you might want to learn to play the guitar, flute, chord organ, or some other instrument. Inexpensive courses may be available from music stores or adult education programs or a friend might teach you.

An experienced musician who finds himself or herself housebound may want to teach children or other adults. You can even volunteer your services to some youngster who couldn't otherwise afford lessons. A nearby school might suggest a student who could benefit from such an offer.

Don't forget that singing may be a good outlet for your musical talent, ranging from sing-alongs at home or in a club to church choirs and other groups.

Crafts

There is a wide variety of craft projects available to fit the interest and abilities of almost everyone.

Here are a few suggestions to help you get started:

1. Decoupage.
2. Wood carving.

3. Macaroni craft.
4. Paper or feather flowers.
5. Model kits.
6. Mosaics—using grains, seeds, colored gravel, or tile.
7. Cake decorating.
8. Felt craft.
9. Shell craft.
10. Jewelry making.
11. Woodworking—trivets, birdhouses, wall racks.
12. Origami—Oriental art of folding paper in all kinds of shapes.

Some other crafts you might consider are:

1. Ceramics—pottery making is one of the oldest crafts. It consists of molding clay into a pleasing shape, glazing it, then firing it in a kiln. Contrary to what you may think, it doesn't take a large outlay of cash to begin enjoying ceramics as a hobby. And you don't need your own kiln. Schools, shops handling supplies and offering lessons, or private studios have kilns available for a small fee.

Your best bet is to sign up for a class and learn the basics. Adult education programs, parks and recreation departments, YMCA and YWCA, ceramic hobby shops, and private hobbyists often offer classes.

2. Macrame is an enjoyable hobby and not too difficult once you learn the basic knots. It takes no tools and almost any type of cord will do—from string or yarn to heavy upholstery cord. You can make belts, holders for hanging plants, wall decorations, and many other lovely things.

For the hobbyist who does not wish to make his or her own patterns, there are several books available. Hobby stores usually carry most of the supplies you need and instruction booklets to help you learn the craft.

3. Brass rubbing is done by covering the engraving on brass monument plaques and other objects with a special sturdy white paper and then rubbing the entire surface with a bland waxy crayon, leaving the depressed parts of the engraving white. The rubbings make beautiful wall hangings—some are over five feet

long. Others can be mounted or framed as you would any other picture.

People who enjoy this hobby keep rolls of paper and crayons in their cars so they are prepared if they come across objects that interest them. Scattered throughout the country on old buildings, historical landmarks, and in some old cemeteries are thousands of brass memorials and plaques that offer interesting designs and artwork.

4. Leathercraft is another hobby you might consider. You will need an instruction book, a few tools, and some supplies, which you can obtain from craft and hobby shops or by mail order.

One company offers a few catalogs listing everything you need for designing and making leather handbags, wallets, belts, and much more. Write to the Tandy Leather Company, 2808 Shamrock, Dept. 7, Fort Worth, Tex. 76107.

Needlework, Sewing, Crocheting, and Knitting

Projects in needlepoint, regular embroidery, and crewel are available for the beginner and the more experienced hobbyist in kits, or you can make up your own canvas. Needles, yarn, and canvas are sold separately in department stores, sewing outlets, and variety stores. They usually carry the kits too. And many are available by mail from listings in many women's magazines, hobby magazines, and mail-order catalogs.

A portable sewing machine can be operated by an individual in a wheelchair or by others with varying degrees of disability. Foot switches can be positioned so they can be run by hand, or other adaptions can be made. With the variety of stitches available on the newer models, you can make all kinds of things from clothing, household linens, and curtains to gifts and decorative items.

Crocheting and knitting also offers lots of possibilities for making items of clothing for men, women, or children plus many household and gift items. Simple "granny squares" can be easily learned, or you might want to learn some of the more complicated crocheting or knitting stitches. There's something for everyone with these skills.

Gardening

Before you decide that outdoor gardening is beyond your reach if you are in a wheelchair, consider some suggestions from wheelchair gardeners. One woman does some weeding with tongs while sitting in her chair. For actual digging and planting she gets out of the chair and sits on the ground. If you need help getting into and out of the chair, have someone there to help. If you do manage by yourself, be sure to gather all your tools beforehand. For those of you who can walk around but can't do too much, consider planters on casters, or you can keep outdoor plants that require minimum care in pots or other containers.

If any kind of outdoor gardening is out of bounds, then do consider the wide range of indoor gardening you might enjoy. It doesn't matter if you live in a one-room apartment or a mansion, there are many things you can grow, from a few pots of African violets or herbs on a windowsill to miniature vegetables, flowers, or ornamental plants. There are all kinds of window shelves, flower carts, hanging plants, terrariums, and many lovely containers to put on coffee tables, bedside stands, or on top of the toilet tank.

Then for those who have lots of patience and want something really different there is Bonsai, or the growing of miniature trees. Several books are available including one by Sunset called BONSAI and THE ART OF GROWING MINIATURE TREES, PLANTS, AND LANDSCAPES by Ishimoto. Local garden clubs or nurseries may also be able to assist you.

Bird Watching and Feeding

If you are housebound most of the time, you can spend many happy hours keeping a bird feeder outside your window stocked with the kind of feed recommended for the birds in your area. One woman keeps looking for new species of birds and she and her family have spotted 155 different kinds at the feeder in their yard.

Good binoculars are necessary to see birds at a distance and to be able to identify their markings. A seven by thirty-five mm pair of binoculars gives an adequate magnification. The beginner also needs a bird guide or bird identification book. Be sure the one you select is easy to carry and has good color illustrations, with detailed descriptions of the birds' habits and songs and where the birds are likely to be found. Both experts and beginners enjoy bird listing. Usually they see how many birds they can spot, identify, and list in one day of bird watching.

You can attract birds to your home by planting ornamental trees, shrubs, and flowers. Providing birdhouses, birdbaths, and feeding stations makes your yard a haven they will enjoy. You can obtain information and the proper food from pet stores and other places that handle birds. There are also many books available from bookstores, libraries, and pet shops.

The National Audubon Society will send you a list of the Audubon groups in your state, along with leaflets about the Society and membership information. If you wish to join, you will have the opportunity to participate in environmental societies through your local chapter. You will also receive the magazine AUDUBON six times a year. For information, write to the National Audubon Society, 950 3rd Avenue, New York, N.Y. 10022.

Photography

Photography is a hobby that can be enjoyed by many people who have restricted mobility or are in wheelchairs. The camera can be placed on a tripod if standing or holding the camera is a problem. If working from a wheelchair, you can hold a tripod in your lap by shortening two of the legs and placing them on each side of you. Lengthen the third leg so it can rest on the floor.

There are several things for the disabled camera enthusiast to consider when choosing a camera. The lenses may be mounted in different ways, since with some cameras it may be too difficult for the person with limited use of his hands to adjust the lens. Be sure to check into this along with all the other considerations of size, weight, and operation. A quadriplegic may have insufficient strength to snap the shutter. An inexpensive shutter release can be held and triggered in the mouth to solve this problem.

There are all kinds of cameras available in a wide range of prices. You might start with an inexpensive one until you decide if this is a hobby you wish to pursue.

You may want to handle your own darkroom work, depending on how avid a photographer you wish to become, if you have a place for one, and if you can manage the job.

Ham Radio, CB, and Shortwave

1. Ham radio can open up a whole new world of contacts all over the globe. It's hard to be bored or lonely when you may talk with an engineer or archeologist in New Guinea, a missionary in the Congo, a student in Moscow, a housewife in Australia, or a botanist in the Galapagos.

The operation of an amateur radio transmitting station is a privilege made available by the Federal Communications Commission to any citizen who can qualify. Granting of a license depends on the person's ability to demonstrate basic technical and code knowledge plus knowing the governing regulations. A person unable to travel may take the FCC examination by mail. There are many disabled ham radio operators including quads, some of whom have worked out ways of adapting equipment to meet their individual needs.

Some amateur radio clubs offer to help any handicapped person become an operator, and some help the individual obtain needed equipment. Instead of buying a new set, you can sometimes purchase a good used set or build one from components. Many electronic shops have instruction books and can help you choose your equipment.

Ham radio involves much more than just idle chatter. It provides a sharing of experiences, joys, sorrows, and opinions with other human beings. Depending on individual desires and interests, it can offer experiences in building equipment, message handling, emergency communications, satellite tracking, and other experiences.

2. Citizen Band radio is also a way of enjoying contact with other people. It is a real asset to the handicapped traveler who has a CB unit in his or her car. It can be used to get help if he or she has an emergency on the road. It can also monitor calls. CB units are not too expensive, and learning to operate them and master-

ing CB jargon are not too difficult. A little practice and you're on your way to becoming an accomplished CBer.

Some electric wheelchair users have CB radios on their wheelchairs. The radios operate from the same batteries which power the electric chairs and enable the users to enjoy the benefits of contact with others.

3. Shortwave listening or DXing is an excellent hobby even for the most severely disabled. There is no technical knowledge needed and no license required. All you need is a radio able to receive the shortwave frequencies.

The Handicapped Aid Program is a private voluntary non-profit organization formed in 1972 for the purpose of introducing the hobby of shortwave listening to the handicapped person.

Shortwave listening broadens the horizons of those who are housebound, offering both entertainment and education. Many countries have programs in English at certain times of the day so you might listen to Radio Israel from Jerusalem or Radio South Africa from Johannesburg. Programs vary with the country and may include news. For information, write to the Handicapped Aid Program, 27 Cleveland Avenue, Trenton, N.J. 08609.

All these hobbies in communications are available to the blind or visually handicapped as well. Books in Braille, on tape, or on records provide much of the instruction for the beginning ham operator. The Braille Technical Press in New York offers courses in radio operation by correspondence. In other areas there are courses available for the blind offered by local ham radio groups.

Pen Pal or Tape Pal Clubs

An escape from boredom or loneliness can be found in pen pal clubs or tape recording clubs. They open up possibilities for new friendships all over the United States and many other countries. People with similar interests share information on hobbies, sports, politics, music, or any subject of interest.

There is a club called International Correspondence Club for the Handicapped. Its basic purpose is to provide means by which disabled persons can become acquainted with others in similar situations. If interested, write to Dick Dobes, 2525 North Broadway, Room 304, Fargo, N.D. 58102.

For those interested in taping, there is the Voicespondence Club, which may be of special interest to the blind who can join for half price. Membership fee for all others is about $5.00. For further information, write to the Voicespondence Club, 2904 State Hill Road F–10, Wyomissing, Penn. 19610.

Art as a Hobby or Career

Many severely disabled people can take up painting, sketching, watercolors, or oils. One artist who had polio learned to use her left hand after losing the use of her right one, which she'd always used before. She tapes old brushes to new ones to extend the length of the handle. She also wedges brushes into the cardboard tubes found on metal coat hangers for added length.

Some people paint by holding brushes in their mouths; others hold the brush between their toes. There is an Association of Mouth and Foot Painting Artists whose members turn out prize-winning and professional work.

Some of these artists are self-taught but most have taken lessons. Available training varies widely from place to place, so you will need to explore what can be found in your area.

Writing Can Be Rewarding

You don't have to be a Hemingway to enjoy writing as a hobby. On man, at eighty-two, who had visual problems, received a typewriter from his daughter, who said, "Dad, would you like to learn to type so you can put on paper some of the stories you've been telling me through the years?"

With his daughter's help he wrote and sold several pieces to local newspapers and magazines. At the age of ninety he still writes an hour or two a day. This gives him both pleasure and satisfaction.

For those of you who aren't interested in having your work published, you can still enjoy keeping a diary or writing a journal. There are now courses offered on journal-keeping, and you might like to try one. However you do it, a journal can be fun. Or you might want to write a family history to give your children or grandchildren.

Bringing Joy to Others

One lady in a wheelchair whose hobby is transcribing for the blind had her husband build her a formica-topped table that fits over her wheelchair so she can work more easily.

One man who is a double amputee wanted to do something for others, so he made dollhouses for the children of some men who were killed in a mine disaster. The children were so pleased he continued building them for others.

If you are still undecided and want more suggestions, a visit to your public library should yield a variety of craft and hobby books for you to consider. Whatever hobby you choose, there is no end to the joys and satisfaction you can bring to yourself and others.

chapter thirteen
TIME OUT FOR PLAY

The old adage "All work and no play makes Jack a dull boy" is true. Everyone needs time out for play. For those of you who were active in sports before an accident or illness, there is a good possibility you can continue with it. Young Ted Kennedy was out on the ski slopes three months after the loss of a leg from bone cancer. There are all kinds of wheelchair games and sports to consider, and for the blind, skiing, swimming, and other sports are possible.

If you were not sports-minded before your accident or illness, there are still lots of other activities to enjoy. Whether you are looking for ways to continue a favorite sport or for a new kind of recreation, the following suggestions and information should offer lots of options for you to consider.

Sports

1. Basketball—One young man from Oregon who has worn an artificial leg since he was five, plays varsity basketball with his high school team.

Wheelchair basketball in the United States began at Birmingham General Army Hospital in Van Nuys, California, in

1946. John D. Old, sportswriter for the Los Angeles *Herald Express*, talked his paper into underwriting a flying national tour of the Birmingham team. Jim Nugent of the University of Illinois organized the first wheelchair basketball tournament in 1949. Wheelchair basketball tournaments have been part of the sports scene ever since.

2. Baseball—One young girl played on a championship softball team and helped her team win the game. This girl catches and throws with one hand almost as fast as others do with two. All this despite the fact she was born with no left arm and was fitted with her first artificial arm when she was two.

Obviously you won't be aiming for pro baseball, but many a sandlot game, school, or recreation club game can provide the opportunity to play despite a handicap.

One innovation in baseball—the beep—has made it possible for the blind to participate in this much-loved game. A beep has been added to the crack of the bat. The baseball has a device implanted in it that emits a beeping sound the batter hears as the ball is pitched. By perceiving the position and travel of the ball, the batter can swing the bat to hit the ball.

Other beep-ball games have been invented, including beep hockey and beep golf.

3. Tennis—Wheelchair tennis has been added to the sports scene. The first annual Wheelchair Tennis Tournament in California was held in Hollywood and was sponsored by the Los Angeles Department of Parks and Recreation. Players are allowed two bounces before returning a shot, otherwise the standard rules are unaltered. A paraplegic recreation assistant for the Department started the program. With the help of an interested tennis instructor, they began teaching people in wheelchairs to play tennis. A rehabilitation center or therapeutic recreation program through your local department of parks and recreation may have such a program going, or perhaps you could suggest such a program if there isn't one near you.

Table Tennis can also be enjoyed by many handicapped persons, including some high level quadriplegics who play with the paddle secured to their hand by tape or brace. The Paralyzed Veterans of America sports activities include competition games.

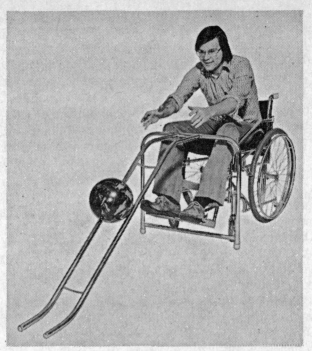

This is one way to go if a ramp will help you make that strike. (Courtesy North American Recreation, Bridgeport, Connecticut.)

4. Bowling—Being confined to a wheelchair is no reason why you can't enjoy the sport of bowling with your friends and family. The first thing to do is to find a bowling alley that is usable. Most bowling lanes do not provide the room between the seats or the level approach to the lanes that is needed by wheelchair bowlers. In some places where wheelchair bowlers go, the managers have put in ramps and made the bathroom doors larger. Some have adaptive bowling equipment available.

Bowling teams may consist of both handicapped and nonhandicapped members. The American Wheelchair Bowling Association can help the wheelchair bowler in getting started, entering league play, or winning a tournament. Various devices are now manufactured for the more seriously disabled bowler. These include the snap-handle ball and stick bowling, both of which can

On the mark! Get set! He scores a hit with this one. (Courtesy George H. Synder, Fort Lauderdale, Florida.)

be used in competition. These two devices are excellent for those with limited grip. Chute bowling, which is actually a movable chute for delivery of the ball, is for the very seriously disabled or muscularly uncoordinated. Chute bowling cannot be used in competition, but works fine for recreational purposes.

There is a ninety-six-page soft cover book covering instructions for wheelchair bowling entitled: WHEELCHAIR BOWLING. It can be ordered from Wheelchair Bowlers of Southern California, 6512 Cadiz Circle, Huntington Beach, Calif. 92647.

BOWLING ORGANIZATIONS American Wheelchair Bowling Association, 2635 NE 19th Street, Pompano Beach, Fla.

Strike! The "third hand" makes for scoring. His wheelchair doesn't slow him down. (Courtesy George H. Snyder, Fort Lauderdale, Florida.)

33062—A packet of information is available from the AWBA including suggested league rules, how to bowl from a wheelchair, a design for a bowling stick, and a history of wheelchair bowling.

Many local parks and recreation departments sponsor handicapped bowling through their therapeutic recreation service.

SPECIAL BOWLING EQUIPMENT Bowling Ball Holder-Ring, George H. Snyder, 5809 NE 21st Avenue, Fort Lauderdale, Fla. 33308—A third hand for the wheelchair bowler. Safely holds the bowling ball while you push up to the foul line to bowl. Made

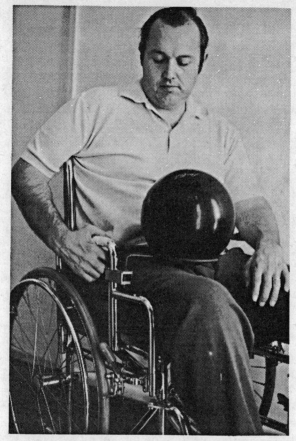

Third hand for wheelchair bowlers. Safely holds ball while moving chair up to foul line. ⅝" diameter steel ring and heavy duty aluminum attachment. No nuts or bolts. Attaches to most chairs. (Courtesy George H. Snyder, Fort Lauderdale, Florida.)

in one piece with no nuts or bolts to lose. This holder is easy to attach to most wheelchairs.

5. Swimming—Opportunities for swimming range in scope from a home swimming pool, the neighborhood swimming hole in river or lake, to an Olympics-size pool. For the newly injured or new swimmer in the disabled class, a variety of aids can help you

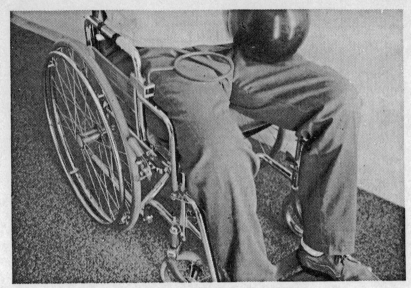

This wheelchair bowler finds the "third hand" attachment makes this sport easier for him to enjoy. (Courtesy George H. Snyder, Fort Lauderdale, Florida.)

get going. Life jackets, rubber rafts, and arm floats can prove useful in developing skills. Some YMCA's and YWCA's offer swimming programs for the handicapped. Check your area for programs available.

Competition swimming is available with several national or state associations for the physically handicapped.

6. Skiing—Skiing technqiues for amputee skiers were developed by two groups in the early fifties. They made outriggers, specially adapted ski poles that are a cross between a crutch and a mini ski and that enable a person standing on one leg to balance and maneuver better than on standard poles. With these adapted poles, amputees are able to ski.

National Inconvenienced Sportspersons Association (NISA) is the largest organization in the country interested primarily in skiing for the handicapped. It was first chartered as the National Amputee Skier's Association in 1967 by a group of Sacramento, California, ski enthusiasts. In 1972 they changed the organization's name to NISA to reflect the change of emphasis in its programs. There are chapters in eight states. For information, write to the Handicapped Sportspersons Association of Sacramento California, 3738 Walnut Avenue, Carmichael, Calif. 95608.

HANDICAPPED SKI PUBLICATIONS

1. KICK THE HANDICAP—LEARN TO SKI, William E. Stieler, Correspondent Adapted Sports Association, 6832 Marlette Road, Marlette, Mich. 48453—A thirty-nine-page book with sections on the history of amputee skiing, information on several ski programs for the disabled,

A fine putt! Al Benson, co-chairman of the Southern California Amputee Golf Association, in action at the Southern California Golf Tournament. (Photograph by Robert Angus.)

and lists of ski areas with special equipment for amputee skiers.
2. Douglas Pringle, President, National Inconvenienced Sportsperson's Association, 3738 Walnut Avenue, Carmichael, Calif. 95608—These instructional manuals for skiing are available.
   a. NATIONAL AMPUTEE SKI TECHNIQUE
   b. TEACHING THE BLIND TO SKI
3. Department of Rehabilitation, Children's Hospital, Denver, Colo. 81026—Each week in Winter Park, Colorado, more than 225 handicapped kids and adults are enrolled in ski classes. Instruction is available for the blind, deaf, paraplegics, those with cerebral palsy, post polio, multiple sclerosis, and spina bifida. There are 100 specially trained instructors; many of them are physical therapists. No handicapped person has ever been refused lessons at Winter Park. Summer programs in hiking, backpacking, float trips, fishing, sailing, and arts and crafts are also at Winter Park. Summer programs in hiking, backpacking, float trips, fishing, sailing, and arts and crafts are also available.

   An excellent twenty-minute movie on the Winter Park Handicapped Skiing Program, entitled *Two . . . Three . . . Fasten Your Ski* is available to groups by writing to the address listed above.

   SKIING ORGANIZATIONS
   United States Ski Association, P.O. Box 66014, AMF O'Hare, Chicago, Ill. 60666
   American Blind Skiing Foundation, 610 South William Street, Mount Prospect, Ill. 60056—The American Blind Skiing Foundation is a national organization chartered in the state of Illinois. Its purpose is to provide an educational skiing program for every interested blind or partially sighted person. Its pilot program was launched in the Chicago area in 1972. In addition to the Chicago program, there are blind skiing organizations in Michigan, Wisconsin, and Indiana, which are supported by ABSF. There is also the Winter Park, Colorado, program mentioned above.

7. Golf—Golf is a game that can be played whether you are in a back or leg brace or are missing an arm or leg. There are several amputee golf associations. Among them are The National Amputee Golf Association, Western International Amputee Golf Association, and the Southern California Amputee Golf Association. For further information, write to Al Benson, Amputee Golf Association, 1424 Lemon Avenue, El Cajon, Calif. 92020.

8. Hockey—Detecting a player's approach from behind by feeling vibrations in the ice is one of the tricks youngsters who are handicapped in hearing learn in the hockey course offered by the

It's all in the balance. A long drive at the Southern California Golf Tournament. (Photograph by Robert Angus.)

American Hearing Impaired Hockey Association. They offer scholarships to young players aged twelve to twenty-two living anywhere in the country; they must have some ice hockey experience and be supplied with basic hockey equipment. To apply, write to the American Hearing Impaired Hockey Association, 1143 West Lake Street, Chicago, Ill. 60607.

9. Archery—Archery is a diversified sport for the target shooter, hunter, or bow-fisherman. For best results, go to an

Lining up a shot at the annual Southern California Golf Tournament. (Photograph by Robert Angus.)

archery shop and test different equipment so you can buy the correct bow and arrows of proper length. If you hunt with a bow and arrow, be sure to check your state's laws and regulations.

Membership in the National Archery Association includes a subscription to ARCHERY WORLD magazine, which includes many ideas on techniques and equipment. The competitive field is well stocked with wheelchair meets or NAA-sanctioned meets. Write to the National Archery Association, Ronks, Penn. 17572.

10. Bicycling—People who are blind or deaf, as well as those with other handicaps, can enjoy bicycling. For those who do not have full vision or complete muscular control, there is a frame that connects two bicycles, so one person can guide both. For information on the buddy bike frame, write to W. L. Romen, Box 455, Saint John, Kans. 67576.

Two racers zoom toward the finish line in one of the exciting races of the National Wheelchair Olympics held in June 1977 at DeAnza College, Cupertino, California. (Courtesy Department of Parks and Recreation, San Jose, California.)

11. Horseback riding is helping many handicapped children and adults to learn new skills and improve muscular control. In centers across the country coordinated by North American Riding for the Handicapped Association, people with physical and emotional handicaps are getting special exercise on horseback. Programs vary from place to place, are under the direction of a physical therapist, and are approved by a physician. For more information, write to the North American Riding for the Handicapped Association, Box 100, Ashburn, Va. 22001.

12. Wheelchair Square Dancing—A thirty-minute cassette giving instructions for wheelchair square dancing is available from Colorado Wheelers, 525 Meadowlark Drive, Lakewood, Colo. 80226.

13. Wheelchair Games—National Wheelchair Games competitions offer a number of sports, including weightlifting, table tennis, archery, swimming, and track and field events. To be eligible to compete in the National Games, one must have a physical

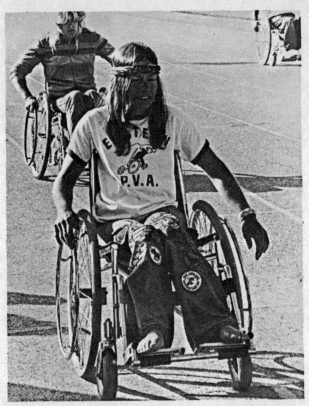

With patches on her jeans and wheels spinning, Natalie Bacon is the lead in the June 1977 National Wheelchair Olympics in Cupertino, California. (Courtesy Department of Parks and Recreation, San Jose, California.)

disability and must have qualified at one of the regional competitions.

Except for weightlifting and swimming, everyone must compete in a wheelchair to standardize competition, although not everyone who competes in the games uses a wheelchair in daily living. Also, men and women compete separately. The competitors are divided into different levels of ability, so that a quadriplegic is not competing against someone whose disability is an amputated leg. For information, write to the National Wheelchair Athletic Association, 40-24 62nd Street, Woodside, N.Y.

The Paralyzed Veterans of America also has a program called Recreational and Competitive Wheelchair Sports. For information, write to Sports Coordinator, Paralyzed Veterans of America, Incorporated, 7315 Wisconsin Avenue, Suite 301-W, Washington, D.C. 20014.

For information on competitive sports for cerebral palsy victims, write to U.C.P. Association of Connecticut, One State Street, New Haven, Conn. 06511.

The California Wheelchair Athletic Association was incorporated in 1968 under the nonprofit laws in the state of California. It is dedicated to the social development, physical activity, and fitness of persons who have physical limitations confining them, partially or wholly, to the use of a wheelchair. Support for CWAA has come from many individuals, but also largely from the outstanding and unselfish support of the city of San Jose through its Parks and Recreation Department, Therapeutic Recreation Services. For information, write to the California Wheelchair Athletic Association, 260 Monticello Drive, Walnut Creek, Calif. 94595. Or write to San Jose Parks and Recreation Department, 151 West Mission Street, Room 203, San Jose, Calif. 95110.

Camping

There are special daycare or resident camps for the handicapped, or you can go camping with family or friends. Choose your campsite carefully. It must have enough level space and be on reasonably solid ground for you to get around easily, especially if you are in a wheelchair. You need a site large enough to move from fire to table to sleeping bag without boulders or drop-offs. Soft dirt can be a hazard to canes, crutches, or wheelchairs. One camping enthusiast suggests camping early in the year while the ground is damp enough to be fairly solid. If you are stuck with soft earth anyway, lay a tarp across the vital living area and stake it tightly. It will give you better traction and keep the area cleaner. Use chalk marks to map underlying rocks or holes.

Carrying a large plastic jug of water can save many trips to faucet or creek. A portable potty can also be a great convenience if the toilets are quite a distance away from your site or if they are not accessible.

The National Easter Seal Society publishes a comprehensive GUIDE TO SPECIAL CAMPING PROGRAMS. Written by authorities in the field, the GUIDE provides a basic reference for organizations involved in planning programs for the handicapped whose needs cannot be met in conventional camping programs.

Although written with primary focus on resident camps for the physically handicapped, the publication contains basic guidelines for day camps as well as camps serving other disability groups.

For information on Easter Seal camps, contact your local Easter Seal Society or write to the National Easter Seal Society, 2023 West Ogden Avenue, Chicago, Ill. 60612.

The year-round Christian camping and retreat center, free of architectural barriers, has special weeks for handicapped campers. Write to Inspiration Center, Christian League for the Handicapped, Box 98, Walworth, Wis. 53184.

ORGANIZATIONS   Committee for the Promotion of Camping for the Handicapped, 2056 South Bluff Road, Traverse City, Mich. 49684.

Fishing

Fishing is a sport that can be enjoyed by individuals with a wide variety of physical handicaps. One device on the market is the Fishing-Aid Rodholder that clamps securely to a pier or boat. It is completely unbreakable and holds the rod firmly so the individual with weak hands or one arm can reel in his or her own catch. For information, write to George C. Vargas, Vargas Fishing-Aid Rodholder Company, 5453 Norwalk Boulevard, Whittier, Calif. 90601.

Hunting and Shooting

For those who don't want to hunt game or travel over rough terrain, trapshooting may be the answer. Individuals in wheelchairs can pursue this sport more readily than field shooting.

Each state has its own rules and regulations for game hunting. You will need to check your area for hunting seasons, license requirements, and other pertinent information.

For those of you who want to hunt game, there is one gadget on the market that might be helpful. If you can use only one arm, you can shoot and hunt again with any size rifle or shotgun. Gun-Support, a devise that can be used by any age person, sitting or standing, indoors or outdoors, weighs just two pounds and is easily adapted to any caliber rifle or any gauge shotgun. For further information, contact Gun-Support, P.O. Box 191, Comes, Tex. 78535.

Games and Puzzles

For those of you who enjoy games and puzzles, there's a wonderful variety to choose from—chess, checkers, all kinds of card games, bingo, and lots of others. They come with large letters for those with visual problems and with giant size playing pieces for those who can't grasp small objects. There are card holders, automatic shufflers, magnetic chess and checkers, spring-loaded billiard cues, plus many other devices adapted for the handicapped. For a list of games and where you can purchase them, see the sources listed at the end of this chapter.

There are electronic challengers which offer computerized games that challenge you. You can play against the computer, allowing you to sharpen your skills, improve your game, and play whenever you want. Chess, checkers, backgammon, and bridge challengers are available.

GAME ROOM CATALOG, a catalog full of fun things to do and great games to play is available from GAME ROOM CATALOG, P.O. Box 4290, Washington, D.C. 20012.

There is a United States Blind Correspondence Chess Champ Tournament book now available. Also there is a publication in Braille named CADYLE, which deals with chess for blind people. To order a subscription of either, write to Gintautas Burba, 30 Snell Street, Brockton, Mass. 02401.

Sightseeing

The following is a small sampling of places that are wheelchair accessible. There are many other places throughout California and the rest of the country that are accessible to wheelchair visitors.

A. The San Diego Wild Animal Park with its 200 different types of animals from Africa and Asia is accessible. The monorail trip takes you on a five-mile safari into the animal's natural habitat. Each monorail has one wheelchair space in front. The only area that might be difficult for a wheelchair is the hill leading to the gorillas and the Birds of Prey Show. The restrooms and eating places are all accessible.

One interesting place at the park is the garden for the visually handicapped. The garden walk is lined with many different varieties of plants and shrubs. Blind visitors are urged to touch and smell. Braille plaques bearing name and information accompany each plant. Tours can also be arranged.

B. Also in southern California there is the Scripps Institute of Oceanography at LaJolla, which has installed ramps within their aquarium. Handicapped persons can now visit virtually all the exhibits, including the tide pool ones.

C. In Los Angeles there is a special garden tailored for the needs of blind students. Created by more than fifty gardeners throughout southern California, it was donated by the group to the Braille Institute, 741 North Vermont Avenue, Los Angeles, Calif.

The garden features plants selected for both sensory stimuli and tactile interest, including lemon scented eucalyptus, natal plum, podocarpus trees, and ivy ground cover.

D. Disney World in Lake Buena Vista, Florida, is ramped for access, and at least fifteen of the major adventures can be enjoyed in a wheelchair. Officials recommend a companion because the place is very large. If you only need a wheelchair because of difficulty walking, you can rent one by the day at the park entrance. Disney World is open every day of the year with special attractions on holidays.

E. The Marriott's Great America Entertainment Parks have wheelchairs for rent at the entrances. Many of the rides, shops, restaurants, and other facilities are wheelchair accessible.

F. For the past several years visitors using wheelchairs have been offered daily tours at the Cave National Park in Kentucky.

They can descend to the caves by elevator and take a two-hour trip in dry passageways through the gypsum crystaline formations known for their fantastic shapes.

G. People with disabilities who visit the White House can go directly to the northeast gate for prompt attention. Wheelchairs may be borrowed for the tour. From the gate and throughout the lower floor and the grounds all paths and floors are fully accessible. Groups can arrange special tours, and there are tours conducted by guides who know sign language.

Many state and national parks are accessible to the handicapped and many touch-and-feel rooms are available for blind visitors to enjoy. Others have touch-and-see trails with signs in Braille, and some also have large print signs for the partially sighted. If you want to know which of the national parks are accessible, write for the publication entitled NATIONAL PARK GUIDE FOR THE HANDICAPPED (stock #2405-0286), Superintendent of Documents, U.S. Government Printing Office, Washington, D.C. 20402.

Cultural Activities

More and more cultural activities are being made accessible to the handicapped. The DeYoung Museum in San Francisco's Golden Gate Park has docents who are able to converse with the deaf in sign language.

Mary Biddle Duke Gallery, North Carolina Museum of Art, founded in 1964, had one of the first "tactile" art exhibitions, which made it possible for visually impaired persons to experience art through touch.

Eugene O'Neill Memorial Theater Center, Waterford, Connecticut, supports three programs for deaf persons.

The Nevil Gallery for the Blind and Sighted, Philadelphia, Pennsylvania, has handrails for visually impaired persons, Braille labeling, and playable musical instruments from several nations.

A museum at Harvard University has a collection of ancient art objects from the Near East, which can be touched and experienced. Interpreters for deaf persons are available to act as guides.

In addition to museums and art galleries, there may be plays, concerts, and other events you can attend. Check the buildings in your area. If they are not accessible, maybe you can start a campaign to make them so. Meanwhile, don't overlook things like open-air concerts in parks, programs offered at high schools or colleges, lectures at churches, hotels, or other public buildings that may be accessible.

Special Programs

Some special programs are available in some YMCA's or YWCA's for swimming and other physical fitness programs. In areas built long before accessibility was required, it may be impossible to get into the buildings, but many of these are raising funds to make their buildings available. So do check on what's being done in your area.

As was mentioned earlier, there are several therapeutic recreation programs available through local parks and recreation departments. One department has a handicapped leisure center as part of its program. It offers arts and crafts, discussion groups, gardening, cooking, excursions, and special events with other educational and therapeutic services whenever there is a need.

The Easter Seal Society sponsors several programs for the handicapped as do other organizations including rehabilitation centers. There are other programs offered by various groups and organizations for those confined to nursing homes or other long-term care facilities. If you don't have recreational facilities available where you live, why not contact one of these groups and see if a program could be started?

Product Listing and Sources

1. ADL CATALOG
   Cleo Living Aids, 3957 Mayfield Road, Cleveland, Ohio 44121
   A. Magnetic chess set—Magnetized chessmen are 2⅝ inches high. Cling to hand-screened linen covered "magneta" board under all conditions.
   B. Magnetic checkers set—Black and natural wooden checkers each with permanent magnet. Folding leatherette board, 9 by 9 inches.
   C. Turntable Scrabble with waffle-grid board—Waffle-grid plastic surface holds either wood or plastic Scrabble tiles. Built-in de-

vice permits board to revolve easily on any flat surface without separate turntable.
D. Magnetic travel Scrabble—Durable enameled steel box 4½ inches by 8 inches. Ivory plastic tiles with imbedded magnets. Box opens flat to serve 8-by-8-inch playing board.
E. Nonmagnetic "pegboard" travel Scrabble—Ivory-colored plastic tiles have socket to fit "pegs" molded on rigid 8¾-by-8¾-inch board.
F. Solitaire master board—Keeps cards in place while playing solitaire in any of 150 ways explained in 128-page game book. Book and deck of cards comes with board.
G. Crossword puzzle board Set—Decorated writing board contoured for easy writing in bed or chair. Includes crossword puzzle dictionary, pencil sharpener, and sample crossword puzzle.
H. Magnetic Kling steel playing cards—Kling cards shuffle, deal, and handle like ordinary cards but "kling" to playing board equipped with concealed permanent magnets. Cards are plastic coated.
I. Three-tier card holder—Device holds up to sixty cards elevated and tilted to keep every card in sight. Cards easily removed.
J. One-hand card shuffler—Rugged to withstand years of use. Takes up to three decks.
K. Bingo card game—Ingenious metal slides do away with easy-to-lose markers. Prevents mistakes. Numbers easier to check.
L. Cleo weaving loom—Regular 7-inch square loom with needle and instruction sheet. All color nylon loops available.
M. Hand loom kit—Overall width—17½ inches, depth—18 inches, height—13 inches. Weaving width—14 inches. Weave up to twenty-four ends to the inch. Metal warp release key.
2. A-Z Industries, 18812-5 Bryant Street, Northridge, Calif. 91324
A. Hot-Shot—Spring-loaded billiard cue. If you can aim a cue, you can play expertly.
3. Blind Foundation, 15 West 16th Street, New York, N.Y. 10011
A. Cards with large print.
4. Creative Playthings, Inc., Princeton, N.J. 08540, or 5757 West Century Boulevard, Los Angeles, Calif. 90045
A. Many types games and products.
5. Fashion Able, Rocky Hill, N.J. 05553
A. Automatic card shuffler—Permits one-hand operation. Handles up to three decks. High-impact plastic frame.
6. Fidelity Electronics, Ltd., 8800 NW 36th Street, Miami, Fla. 33178
A. Computerized games—Microprocessor-based games for playing checkers, chess, bridge, or backgammon. Also a voice chess challenger. These games are widely available at Sears Roebuck and Company, Montgomery Ward, and J. C. Penney. If you can't find them in your area, write directly to the company.

7. Handee Products Company, 2401 Victoria Drive SW, Cedar Rapids, Iowa 52404
   A. Pool Handicapper—For those who need a steady shot to play pool. Unit may be used in any position. Allows you to shoot any conceivable shot with same ease as two-handed player.
8. North American Recreation, P.O. Box 758, Bridgeport, Conn. 06001
   A. Height-adjustable billiard, tennis, and shuffleboard tables.
   B. Handle-grip bowling ball—Handle snaps back on release.
   C. Uni-Que—Aluminum spring-loaded billiard cue.
   D. Bowling ball ramp.
   E. Ring toss.
   F. Rubber horse shoes.
   G. Many more items available.
9. Zodiac of North America, Inc., 11 Lee Street, Annapolis, Md. 21401
   A. Rubber boats.

Many department stores also carry large print playing cards and some of these other devices.

chapter fourteen
PRODUCTS FOR THE HANDICAPPED

Everybody likes to find new ideas, products, or services that can make life easier, save time and energy, or make it possible to accomplish a desired goal. The handicapped may have to look a bit harder because the things they might find useful are not always so widely advertised.

Some of these products are new on the market, whereas others are not. We have listed more than one source for many items, so that you can compare prices and can shop around for the features that best meet your individual needs.

Categorized products are listed first, followed by catalogs that offer a wide variety of products for the disabled.

Aids to Daily Living

1. Bathing Aids to the Handicapped, P.O. Box 1956, Greeley, Colo. 80631—Portable inflatable tub—no lifts or lifting needed. Individual rolls onto deflated tub, which is then inflated and filled with water. Tub is 21 by 60 inches by 8½ inches in depth (inside dimensions).
2. Comfort-Able Aids, Box 275, Somerset Street, Raritan, N.J. 08869—Doorknob helper—For arthritics and others with limited finger dexterity. Rubber lever fits over a standard doorknob so a mere downward push releases the latch.

3. Conair Corporation, 11 Executive Avenue, Edison, N.J. 08817—The Wiz—enables individuals with use of only one hand to style their own hair more easily. Device includes round brush, air concentrator, fine tooth comb, wide tooth comb detangler, and pick-and-lift attachment.
4. HB and D Products, Box 743, South Laguna, Calif. 92677—Leisure reader—holds your paperback book in perfect reading position and turns pages with the slightest touch.
5. Holo Industries, 11602 Lampson Avenue, Garden Grove, Calif. 92640—Lift-transporter—gives patient complete independence in getting in and out of bed from wheelchair.
6. H. Hutson, P.O. Box 1415, Denver, Colo. 80201—Un-Skru—opens any screw cap bottle or jar in three seconds. Mounts on wall or underneath cabinet.
7. Lumex, Inc., 100 Spence Street, Bay Shore, N.Y. 11706—Tub tricks—bathtub safety rail with double handhold permits patient to support himself or herself whether sitting or standing. Will not mar the tub finish nor require special tools or permanent fastening to the tub.
8. Neil Henson Company, P.O. Box 132, Jackson, Mo. 63755—Remote-control switch—requires no installation. Turns on or off any household device up to 300 watts at a distance of up to one hundred feet.
9. Nelson Medical Products, 5690 Sarah Avenue, Sarasota, Fla. 33581—New type weighing system—use on most bathroom scales. Unfold and place over scales, ready to use. Individual may weigh him or herself.
10. Charles Parker Company, 290 Pratt Street, Meriden, Conn. 06450—Folding shower chair—has two-inch thick cushion.
11. Pentalic Corporation, 132 West 22nd Street, New York, N.Y. 10011—Perfect bookmark—hidden spring mechanism holds each page back as you read.
12. Rayl Distributing Company, Box 321, Russelville, Ind. 46979—Easy switch—operates lamps, radios, TV's, buzzers, almost anything by the lightest touch of any part of the body. No special wiring; simply plug in.
13. Richline Company, Inc., 2515 Pilot Knob Road, St. Paul, Minn. 55120—Pocket pal—useful to those who have trouble stooping or reaching. Extends to 17 inches and will pick up seven-ounce piece of metal.
14. Spenco Medical Corporation, Box 8113, Waco, Tex. 76710—Spenco cushions—provide comfort and protection from wheelchair pressure sores and sitting fatigue. Covered with velour fabric or naugahyde. Cushion will not leak and is easily cleaned.

15. The Left Hand, 145 East 27th Street, New York, N.Y. 10016—Left-hand products—including pens, playing cards, wallets, watches, cameras, drinking cups, etc.

Mobility

1. American Stair-Glide Corporation, 4001 East 138th Street, Grandview, Mo. 64030—Porch-lift—wheelchair lift, easily installed at porch landing side of a stairway or at the end of stairway. Operates on household current.
2. ANIK, Inc., P.O. Box 3232, San Rafael, Calif. 94901—Personal mobility aid—adjustable to person's height, used as a walker or three-point cane. Easily dismantled for transportation.
3. E.F. Brewer Company, P.O. Box 159, Menomonee Falls, Wis. 53051—Portascoot—single motor, front wheel drive offers two forward speeds and reverse. Easy to drive and maneuver, makes traveling a joy.
4. Burke Enterprises, P.O. Box 1064, Mission, Kans. 66222—Elevating recliner—will raise you to your feet and lower you back into your chair. Will also recline to a comfortable position.
5. Cheney Company, 3015 South 163rd Street, New Berlin, Wis. 53151—Wheelchair lift—designed to carry a person in a wheelchair from one floor to another. Will fit on stairway as narrow as 36 inches.
6. Earl's Stairway Lift, 2513ACI Center Street, Cedar Falls, Iowa 50613—Wheelchair lift—May be used as a porch stairway or 35-inch inside stairway. Platform may be folded so stairway can be used for normal use.
7. Easy Riser, 87 Millstone Road, Wilton, Conn. 06897—Easy riser—can raise height of any chair to your comfort zone.
8. Handi-Ramp, Inc., P.O. Box 745, 1414 Armour Boulevard, Mundelein, Ill. 60060—Portable ramp channels—nonskid wheelways, sturdy construction, safety wheel guides.
9. Independent Transfer Equipment Company, 11602 Knott, Suite 9, Garden Grove, Calif. 92641—Patient transfer lift—motorized both vertically and horizontally for independent operation by the handicapped individual.
10. Industrial Research and Engineering, Inc., 2409 N. Kerby, Portland, Oreg. 97227—Aqualift—swimming pool lift. Patient can get into and out of swimming pool by his or herself.
11. Monadnock Lifetime Products, Inc., Fitzwilliam, N.H. 03447—Ice gripper—help to those who must use cane or crutches in icy weather. Easily retractable to eliminate damage to indoor floors. Chrome-plated.

12. Nelson Medical Products, 5690 Sarah Avenue, Sarasota, Fla. 33581—Push-matic folding walker—simple pressure does it—no knobs. Quick height change with pushbutton adjustment.
13. Ortho-Kinetics, P.O. Box 2000, Waukesha, Wis. 53187—Cushion lift-chair—lifts you slowly and safely to your feet.
14. Piper Brace Sales Corporation, 811 Wyandotte Street, Kansas City, Mo. 64105—Folding metal crutch—folds up to 22 inches for easy storage. When open, adjustable for persons up to 6½ feet tall.
15. Shylar Corporation, P.O. Box 1478, Colorado Springs, Colo. 80901—Wilson transporter—transfer from bed to chair to bathroom with a fraction of the effort and time once required, and without lifting or carrying.
16. Stanley Magic Door, Farmington, Conn. 06032—Silent swing—automatically opens and closes doors with push of a button. Easily installed on interior doors at home, at work, or in public buildings.

Transportation

1. American Adaptive Systems Corporation, 3651 Sausalito Street, Los Alamitos, Calif. 90720—Lift-a-way wheelchair lift—wheelchair ties down. Power seat. For vans.
2. Amigo Sales, Inc., 6693 Dixie Highway, Bridgeport, Mich. 48722—Lightweight electric vehicle—use instead of wheelchair. Narrow enough to go through most doorways. Two forward speeds and reverse, foot brakes, low center of gravity. Powered by twelve-volt electric motor and battery.
3. Besam Automatic Door Operators, Besam, Incorporated, P.O. Box 2197, 338 Knowlton Street, Bridgeport, Conn. 06608—Door openers—open doors from lightweight interior doors in home to larger sliding doors in a public building. Activated by a variety of controls.
4. Braun Corporation, 1014 South Monticello, Winamac, Ind. 46996—Vans for immediate conversion—mini-top, 64 inches headroom; high top, 74 inches headroom. Raised doors, swing or sliding. Fully or semi-automatic lift. Power seat and doors. Complete line of driving aids. Mini-motor homes available.
5. Cameron Enns Company, 13637 South Madsen Avenue, Kingsburg, Calif. 93631—Foot controls for cars, steering accomplished by either leg, other leg operates brake and throttle. Custom-made to fit each individual. Adaptable to motor homes, vans, and trucks, and the 1979 Rabbit and Ford Fairmont.
6. Die-a-Matic, Inc., 4004 5th Road, North, Arlington, Va. 22203—German foot controls—foot control system modified for Volkswagen Rabbit. Everything, including radio, lights, windshield wiper can be operated by foot or knee. Steering accomplished by moving the pedal.

7. Drive-Master Corporation, 16 Andrews Drive, West Paterson, N.J. 07424—Hand controls—adaptable to most automatic transmission automobiles.
8. Fred Scott and Sons, 1444 W. Rand Road, Des Plaines, Ill. 60016—Translift unit—offers rear door loading of wheelchair into vans. Also has Inval-Aid ramps, made of durable corrosive resistant material. Standard lengths—10 feet. Can be folded for easy transportation.
9. Independence Factory, P.O. Box 597, Middleton, Ohio 45042—Loading device—mechanical assistance for getting wheelchair into car.
10. K.G.B. Research and Development, 7025 Duncan Road, Punta Gorda, Fla. 33950—Attendant-operated wheelchair brake—Designed for a small, frail attendant to effortlessly and safely descend ramp with a patient.
11. Mobility Engineering and Development, Inc., 7131 Hayvenhurst Avenue, Van Nuys, Calif. 91406—Push-button van—designed especially for quadriplegics. Features push-button control of all van functions from a panel to the left of driver. Acceleration, braking, and turning are handled by a small, foam-covered steering wheel mounted on a tiller. Van also equipped with wheelchair lift and wheelchair hold-down system, operated from push-button panel.
12. Mobility Products and Designs, Inc., 709 Kentucky Street, Vallejo, Calif. 94590—Manufacturers of MRoss handcontrols—steering devices, left-foot gas pedals, park brake handles, left-hand gear shift levers, right-hand turn signal levers.
13. Owen-Pacific Associates, 412-A Woodward Boulevard, Pasadena, Calif. 91107—Miniwinch—Assists driver in loading chair. Hand-operated, for use on two-door hardtops.
14. Saab Scana of America, Saab Drive, P.O. Box 697, Orange, Conn. 06477—Permobil—in use in Sweden for about twelve years. Can go over curbs, climb hills, and negotiate snow and ice. Can be driven by kids as young as age four, or older persons, or patients with a spinal ailment who have use of their shoulders and upper arms. Battery powered, safe for downtown driving as well as off-road travel.
15. Seton Name Plate Corporation, 949 Boulevard, New Haven, Conn. 06505—Parking clearance sign reading: Please leave five feet clearance. For disabled drivers having difficulty getting into their cars because others are parked too close. Plastic card, securely held in place inside of auto by a raised window.
16. Summit Corporation, P.O. Box 578, Valparaiso, Fla. 32580—Pak-A-Rak wheelchair carrier—attaches to car's rear bumper. Has automatic lock-in mechanism and Pak-A-Jacket for use during bad weather.
17. Tilt-n-Tote Wheelchair Carrier Co., P.O. Box 103, Waterville, Ohio 43566—Unit for carrying a wheelchair at the rear exterior of the

trunk. Rack tilts down so chair can be rolled into place and automatically tilts up and locks into place. Adapts to standard hitches and padlocks for security.
18. Voyager, Inc., Box 1557, South Bend, Ind. 46634—Rugged battery-powered wheelchair for indoor or outdoor use.
19. Wells-Engborg Company, Inc., Box 6388, Rockford, Ill. 61125—Hand-control devices—Write for their brochure.
20. Wheelchair Carrier Sales Corporation, P.O. Box 16202, Phoenix, Ariz. 85011—Electromatic top loader for wheelchairs fits on top of almost any automobile, van, or pick-up, including mini-cars. Powered from your car battery.
21. Wright-Way, Inc., P.O. Box 40907, Garland, Tex. 75040—Hand-control devices for your car. Write for their free brochure.

Communication

Many telephone problems of the disabled can be solved by the local telephone company. Most people, however, are unaware that special telephones are available for the handicapped and all too frequently order a standard telephone with the assumption that the handicapped member of the household will not be able to use it.

Most telephone companies have a marketing coordinator of services for the handicapped who is available for consultation on any problems you may have.

Some devices available from your telephone company are:

A. Tone ringer—concentrates all of the sound energy to frequency range which the majority of persons with impaired hearing can hear.
B. Loud bell—much louder than normal telephone bell.
C. Signals in different frequencies—Signals in various frequencies for persons who have difficulty hearing regular telephone bell.
D. Lamp indicator—visually indicates the phone is ringing.
E. Vis-Com—translates beeps from standard touch-tone telephone into lights on a visual display panel. Links homes of deaf persons with firehouse, police station, or hospital. Allows deaf to "talk" to another deaf person on phone.

1. Applied Communications Corporation, P.O. Box 555, Belmont, Calif. 94002

A. TTY—teletypewriter turns on automatically when phone handset is placed on phonetype cradle.
   B. Phonetype—acoustic link between telephone and teletypewriter.
   C. Monitor light—indicates dial tone, ringing, call answered, or busy signal.
   D. Multipurpose signaler.
   E. Remote control transmitter and receiver.
2. Mark Dahmke, MCD Consulting, 8306 Sellect, 600 North 15th Street, Lincoln, Nebr. 68508
   A. Bionic voice—designed around a computalker consultants CT-1 Speech Synthesizer. Can be operated like a spelling board, without knowledge of computers.
3. Drive Master Corporation, 61-A North Mountain Avenue, Montclair, N.J. 07042
   A. Mobile transceiver unit—disabled drivers having trouble on the road can usually get help with a citizen's band radio using Emergency Channel 9. Unit equipped with push-button changer.
4. Fidelity Electronics, Limited, 5245 West Diversey Avenue, Chicago, Ill. 60639
   A. Fidelity comfort and communication environmental control systems can do the following by a mere puff or sip on a straw:
   Answer and place phone calls.
   Operate a TV set or radio.
   Turn room light off and on.
   Control an electric bed.
5. Harriet Carter, Department 14109, Plymouth Meeting, Penn. 19462
   A. Telephone amplifier—enables you to speak and hear from anywhere in the room. Not necessary to hold the phone.
6. Ortho Kinetics, Inc., P.O. Box 2000, Waukesha, Wis. 53186
   A. Silent Companion—If you need help, Silent Companion is there to automatically call your friends, relatives, doctor, or neighbors. All you need to do is push the tiny remote control you wear. Silent Companion takes over and dials a program of calls to the people you've chosen and delivers a prerecorded message that you need assistance. It continues calling until help arrives.
7. Tele-Sensory Systems, Inc., 3408 Hillview Avenue, Palo Alto, Calif. 94304
   A. Canon Communicator—for nonoral, motor-impaired persons. Letters or symbols are selected on the keyboard and printed on a paper display. Can be worn on wrist.
8. Tele-Tronics United, Inc., 2910 Rubidoux Boulevard, Riverside, Calif. 92509
   A. A new telephone, Sensor touch-dial PortaCall is ideal for disabled persons. Has no pushbuttons; number is entered by

touching each digit. If you get a busy signal, touching the redial button will automatically redial the last number called.

Miscellaneous

1. A.B.L. Associates, 1975 East 65th Street, Cleveland, Ohio 44103

    Strap-loc—simple plastic device attached to the bed rail to keep call lights and TV remote control units within easy reach. Can also be used to support oxygen, drainage, IV, and other tubing.

2. Braun Corporation, 1014 S. Monticello, Winimac, Ind. 46996

    Handi-John—a portable restroom 87 by 61 by 61 inches that allows maximum wheelchair maneuverability. Fiberglass construction, ideal for recreational areas, parks, fairs, and golf courses.

3. Dimensional Graphics, Inc., 222 W. Huron Street, Chicago, Ill. 60610

    Touch-and-know signs—available on pressure-sensitive backing with Braille or tactile lettering.

4. Extensions for Independence, P.O. Box 3754, Downey, Calif. 90242

    A desk with built-in turntables brings equipment and supplies within easy reach.

5. Hawk Enterprises, Inc., P.O. Box 20490, San Jose, Calif. 95160

    Gloves specifically designed for handicapped individuals who depend on their hands for greater mobility. Come in three styles, reinforced with padding on palm and fingertips.

6. MED Laboratories, 7036 Madera Drive, Goleta, Calif. 93107

    E-Z Call—nurse call-switch can be used by almost all patients, even those severely paralyzed or disoriented. Fitted with pair of clips to fasten securely to patient's head, hand, or foot as needed.

7. POSSUM, Inc., 700 North Valley Street, Suite B, P.O. Box 4424, Anaheim, Calif. 92803

    They will provide information about the availability of the POSSUM system in the United States.

8. Smith Corona Operations, Division of SCM Corporation, 831 James Street, Syracuse, N.Y. 13203

    Typewriter with a Dvorak simplified keyboard for the handicapped. One-hand operation, left or right. Also manufactures a cerebral palsy mask which is available on the Coronamatic 2200 model. These special keyboards are manufactured for the Typewriter Institute for the Handicapped. For more information, write the Typewriter Institute for the Handicapped, 3109 West Augusta Avenue, Phoenix, Ariz. 85021.

Catalogs

1. American Foundation for the Blind, Consumer Products Department,

15 West 16th Street, New York, N.Y. 10011—Write for their free catalog listing aids and appliances for the blind and visually handicapped, including watches, clocks and timers, household and personal items, recreation, writing, and communication aids, and medical devices.
2. E.F. Brewer Company, P.O. Box 159, Menomonee Falls, Wis. 53051—Carries shower chairs, walker, walker aids, canes, quadriplegic canes, and much more.
3. Buyers Guide, Accent on Living, P.O. Box 700, Bloomington, Ill. 61701—Buyer's guide of products for the disabled covers personal care, mobility, home management, communications, recreation travel, and much more.
4. Cleo Living Aids, 3957 Mayfield Road, Cleveland, Ohio 44121—Carries crutches, canes, wheelchairs, lap trays, several types of reaching devices, elastic shoe laces, plastic shoe horns, button aids, reading and writing aids, incontinent pants for men and women, recreational equipment, magnetic chess and checker sets, card holders and shufflers and other games, occupational therapy devices, and other rehabilitation aids, including many types of eating utensils.
5. Everest and Jennings, Inc., 1803 Pontius Avenue, Los Angeles, Calif. 90025—Carries wheelchairs, walking aids, canes, crutches, walkers, special pressure-relief cushions, shower chairs and shower/bath benches, bathroom safety aids, toilet safety aids, and other home and rehabilitation equipment.
6. FashionAble, Rocky Hill, N.J. 08553
    A. Easy-on, easy-off clothing for women, dresses, pantsuits, undergarments, and swim suits.
    B. Self-help devices—eating devices and several recreational and communication aids.
    C. Housekeeping aids—easy-wring mops, no-stoop dust pans, brooms, pan handler, tongs, mitts, jar openers, and much more.
7. Lumex, Inc., 100 Spence Street, Bay Shore, N.Y. 11706—Manufacturers of walkers, canes, commodes, and shower chairs. Catalog available.
8. Maddak, Inc., Pequannock, N.J. 07440—Carries self-help aids of various kinds, patient aids, urinary devices, and many others.
9. G.E. Miller, Inc., 484 South Broadway, Yonkers, N.Y. 10705—Suppliers of physical medicine and self-help equipment including stocking and dressing aids, eating utensils, and homemaking equipment.
10. Nelson Medical Products, 5690 Sarah Avenue, Sarasota, Fla. 33583
    A. Patient aids—grab bars, toilet guardrails, folding bed trays, hydraulic bath lifts, wheelchairs, and walkers.
11. Ortho Kinetics, 1610 Pearl Street, Waukesha, Wis. 53187—Carries cushion lift-chairs in several styles, adaptive stander, special care wheelchairs, and a toilet lift.

12. Charles Parker Company, 290 Pratt Street, Meriden, Conn. 06450—Bathroom fixtures of stainless steel including grab bars and other accessories. Especially useful when remodeling or building.
13. Sears Roebuck and Company—Contact the Sears store nearest you for information on ordering and obtaining a catalog.
    A. Wheelchairs—several types available.
    B. Convalescent aids—bed trays, lift chair, on-bed tray.
    C. Protective undergarments and bedding protectors—lined briefs for men, women, and children, bed pad, disposable underpads, plastic draw sheet.
    D. Commodes for sickroom and colostomy needs.
    E. Heating devices—vibrating deep heat massager, heating pads, arthro muff, 36-inch wrap-around heat bandage.
    F. Special problem aids—abdominal and back support, back braces for rigid control, tennis elbow support, shoulder braces.
    G. Hydromassage and steam therapy—compact whirlpool bath, rechargeable thirty-gallon whirlpool bath.
14. Winco Products, Winfield Company, Inc., 3062 46th Avenue North, St. Petersburg, Fla. 33714—Specializes in self-help equipment, including raised toilet seats, shower/commode chairs, walkers, and safety bars.

chapter fifteen
DON'T OVERLOOK THE SPIRITUAL

"Be bold and strong! Banish fear and doubt! For remember, the Lord your God is with you wherever you go."

(Joshua 1:9, The Living Bible)

The Bible

Words of inspiration from the Bible are available in many translations—from the King James Version and the New English Bible to the Living Bible and Good News for Modern Man. Some are eaiser to read and understand than others, so choose the one that seems best for you. Other religious writings are available through your local library.

Hospital chaplains and members of the clergy will find this chapter to be a source of helpful suggestions for their hospitalized patients, for those who are housebound and unable to attend church, and, for those who, for one reason or another, prefer other alternatives for worship and inspiration.

For those with impaired vision, the Bible is available in several large print editions. If your local bookstore does not have one, contact a local organization for the blind to obtain a list of publishers who put out large print editions of the Bible, or write to the Bible Society of America, Park Avenue and 57th Street, New York, N.Y. 10022.

The Bible is available in Braille; it is also available on tape and on phonograph records.

Churches

Many churches are wheelchair accessible and some have pews with amplifiers for the hard-of-hearing. Others have cassettes of sermons, special programs and musicals that can be checked out for use by the housebound. For those unable to attend regular services, some churches have special programs offering spiritual help, Bible study, and opportunity for social contact. A few churches even have vans available that accommodate wheelchairs and provide transportation for those who need it.

Don't be disappointed if your church doesn't meet your needs. You do have other options. First, you can make your needs

The beautiful Garden Grove Community Church of Garden Grove, California, is ideal for car-bound worshippers. Dr. Robert Schuller is the minister. In addition, services are held in the regular sanctuary. (Courtesy Robert Schuller Ministries, Garden Grove, California.)

known. Sometimes the church is not aware of what is needed, and, once informed, it may be willing to provide requested changes. Or, why not visit other churches until you find one that is not only accessible but fulfills your spiritual needs as well?

Many churches sponsor services in nursing homes. If you have a family member in a nursing home that does not have services available, you could request your pastor to initiate one. Sometimes several churches rotate Sundays, each with their musical groups providing music and singing for the patients.

Some large hospitals have chapels offering both Protestant and Roman Catholic services. These chapels might be available to you if you live where there are no accessible churches. They welcome anyone who wishes to attend and are set up for patients in wheelchairs, on stretchers, and on crutches, so there should be no problem in attending.

Drive-in churches are found in some cities from California to Florida. The most widely known is probably the Garden Grove Community Church in California, pastored by Dr. Robert Schuller. Their drive-in sanctuary allows people to enjoy the service while sitting in their cars.

Radio Programs

There are many church and religious programs available on the radio for you to enjoy. Consult your local paper to see what's availabe in your community.

A sampling of programs heard in western United States are Haven of Rest, denominational services, radio stations that broadcast religious programs and music all day, such as KEAR in San Francisco, KEBR in Sacramento, California, KFOX in Long Beach, California, KNIS in Carson City, Nevada, and many more.

To mention a couple in the midwest, there is KYER in Shenandoah, Iowa or WMBI in Chicago, Illinois. Some programs that can be heard in this area are: Bible College of the Air, Sacred Melodies, Grace Worship Hour, Back to the Bible, religious news, and Morning Chapel Hour.

In the East, there is WFME in Newark, New Jersey, or WFSI in Annapolis, Maryland, carrying programs similar to those listed above.

Speakers such as Dr. Robert Schuller, Reverend Billy Graham, and other well-known religious leaders have programs heard from coast to coast.

In many areas these programs are broadcast in Spanish and other languages.

TV Programs

In addition to the radio programs listed above, there are several TV ministries, such as Rex Humbard, Jerry Falwell, Jimmy Swaggart, Oral Roberts, Day of Discovery, and others. You may want to try the different programs until you find one that gives you the combination of ministry and music most uplifting and inspirational.

Bible Study Groups

If you are unable to attend church but would like to participate in a small group, there are many nondenominational Bible study groups that meet in the members' homes. You don't have the problems of sitting on hard pews, meetings too prolonged to sit through, or parking, and often you can get a ride with one of the members if needed.

Prayer Help and Inspiration by Telephone

Whatever your need, day or night, there are several twenty-four-hour prayer groups you can call.

1. The Prayer Tower, Oral Roberts University—(918) 492-7777.
2. The Rex Humbard Prayer Group—(216) 929-8691.
3. Silent Unity—(800) 921-2935 or (816) 524-5104.
4. Foundation for Christian Living, a recorded message by Dr. Norman Vincent Peale—(914) 855-5111.
5. Many local groups have their own recorded messages under headings such as Dial a Prayer, Instant Inspiration, and others.

Inspirational Booklets, Pamphlets, and Magazines

1. Oral Roberts—Books, pamphlets, and monthly publication ABUNDANT LIFE. All publications free. Write to Oral Roberts, Tulsa, Okla. 74171.

2. Rex Humbard—Books, pamphlets, and monthly publication THE ANSWER. All publications free. Write to Rex Humbard, Akron, Ohio 44331.
3. The Foundation for Christian Living—Pamphlets called CREATIVE HELP FOR DAILY LIVING. Write to The Foundation for Christian Living, Pauling, N.Y. 12564.
4. Radio Bible Class—A free monthly booklet OUR DAILY BREAD with Bible quotations and readings for daily family devotions. Write to Radio Bible Class, P.O. Box 22, Grand Rapids, Mich. 49555.
5. The Anchor—a free monthly publication offering a daily Scripture and inspirational message. Write to THE ANCHOR, Haven of Rest Broadcast, Box 2031, Hollywood, Calif. 90028.
6. GUIDEPOSTS—A magazine available by regular monthly subscription. It is not only nondenominational, but is for Protestant, Roman Catholic, and Jewish readers alike. There is also a yearly DAILY GUIDEPOSTS of daily devotions and inspiration available for a modest fee. For further information on either of the above, write to GUIDEPOSTS, Carmel, N.Y. 10512.

There are many others such as CHRISTIAN HERALD, CATHOLIC DIGEST, THE LUTHERAN, and other denominational publications.

The CHRISTIAN HERALD has a family book service that is a book club offering not only Christian books but also books for family reading that avoid the sex and violence found in so many current secular books. Write to the Christian Herald Family Bookshelf, Chappaqua, N.Y. 10514.

In addition, there are numerous Christian bookstores offering a wide variety of inspirational reading and many different versions of the Bible. Many carry records and tapes of Gospel recording artists.

Christian Volunteer Group

A group called The Overcomers now has two chapters in Northern New Jersey and are expanding rapidly. They are a large group of volunteers who meet monthly. They take care of the needs of non-ambulatory people who need help getting to and from the hospital and similar types of services on a one on one basis. They also have a summer camp in Pennsylvania for handicapped people. It is free to those who can't afford to pay. For further information, write to The Overcomers, Al Bonsignore, 269 Golden Gate Avenue, Oradell, N.J. 07649.

Accessible Churches

If you belong to a church that is planning to remodel or to build a new church, there is a booklet of guidelines on constructing barrier-free churches, including diagrams and drawings of everything from parking facilities to the entire church—narthex, sanctuary, and chancel areas, as well as restrooms, telephone and drinking fountain accessibility. Write to the Episcopal Church Building Fund, 815 2nd Avenue, New York, N.Y. 10017.

chapter sixteen
WHAT COMMUNITIES ARE DOING

Many communities now strive to meet the needs of their handicapped members. Recent changes in the laws, federal funding available for some projects, and pressure from handicapped organizations and other groups are all helping to bring about these necessary improvements.

The following are a few samples showing what some communities are doing and pointing up areas that need future change. Perhaps you can compare some of these ideas with what your local community is doing and look for ways to help. One way of doing this is by joining a local handicapped organization and other groups that are working on these issues. Group action often accomplishes more than an individual alone can do.

Transportation

Many communities have transit systems for elderly and disabled persons. One successful system in California consists of thirteen Dodge vans used as small buses. Two are capable of transporting persons in wheelchairs.

The new unit for disabled persons is operated on a first-come, first-served, dial-a-ride basis. Local residents who have identification cards indicating that they would have a difficult time using the normal mass transit may call the system and make reservations.

A city in Florida uses a dozen van-size buses as part of its total transit system. This system incorporates door-to-door service for disabled and elderly persons in its operations.

The interior of the van is flexible. There are three seats which will easily fold up to make room for a wheelchair. Or the van can be adapted for use by wheelchairs only. In one part of the van, there are three higher-than-normal seats for persons with knee and hip problems. The van's roof has been raised to about six feet.

In Ohio, one community's plan includes a small multipurpose bus. Such a bus would accommodate high-density downtown circulation and have low-density suburban and rural demand/response capability, as well as accommodating the special needs of handicapped and elderly passengers.

Another county in California is planning an entire fleet of 516 buses to be refitted with a variety of devices to help the handicapped.

The Metropolitan Transportation Commission covering the nine San Francisco Bay counties is now committed to fully accessible Bay Area public transportation. All buses must be wheelchair accessible or offer equal facilities for the handicapped in the transit operators' service area. Several members of the California Association of the Physically Handicapped, working as advisors to the Commission, were instrumental in the adoption of the policy.

BART (Bay Area Rapid Transit) is a space-age transit system whose silver trains provide fast, efficient transportation around and under the Bay Area in minutes. Perhaps the most exciting part of BART's seventy-one-mile system is the Transbay Tube—the world's longest and deepest underwater tunnel—through which it takes only seven minutes to whisk you from one side of San Francisco Bay to the other.

All BART stations are equipped with special elevators for the handicapped, and the trains are wheelchair accessible. Station agents are usually available to offer assistance to the handicapped.

Public Buildings

SCHOOLS Schools at all levels—from grammar and high schools to colleges—are being made more accessible to the handicapped through alterations and remodeling of present facilities, as the demand for accessibility increases. Hopefully, new ones being built will eliminate architectural barriers in the planning stage.

CHURCHES Many churches are building ramps for wheelchairs and making sanctuaries accessible when possible without expensive remodeling. However, many other churches are slow to see the need to change. This is one area in which more awareness of the needs of the handicapped in the community is needed by ministers, priests, rabbis, church boards, building committees, and anyone who influences church policy and decisions.

HOTELS AND MOTELS Each year large numbers of handicapped people are traveling, and hotels and motels are recognizing the need for accessible accommodations.

Getting ready for the first White House Conference on Handicapped Individuals motivated many hotels and motels in the Washington, D.C., area to modify their rooms, install grab bars in bathrooms, add ramps, lower telephones, and make other necessary changes in bathrooms and other public areas.

The Sheraton Park Hotel and Motor Inn hosted the first such gathering in the nation. The changes made represented a breakthrough for disabled persons desiring to visit the nation's capital or attend conferences there.

The Sheraton Park placed Braille signs outside meeting rooms and elevators and on most elevator control panels. Braille menus have always been available in the restaurants and food service outlets.

STORES Grocery stores with turnstiles, department stores, and pharmacies are just beginning to consider the needs of handicapped customers. A great deal more needs to be done in these areas.

Officials Spend a Day in a Wheelchair

In many areas city and county officials spend a day in a wheelchair to learn what it means to be physically handicapped. They attempt to get in and out of the administration building, try to use its elevators, restrooms, and public telephones. City Hall, welfare offices, and other city and county buildings may also be checked.

Others who may be invited to participate are mayors, city managers, county department heads, building inspectors, public health and social service workers, and the staff of the county architectural section.

Many state and federal groups are making the same kind of study. In Washington, D.C., some government engineers and architects were given a training assignment of being "handicapped for a day." They learned how hard it is to get a wheelchair over a doorsill or across a thick rug. It was almost impossible to get a drink from a drinking fountain. Bathrooms, office desks, and cafeteria tables all presented problems.

Learning first-hand what the problems are is a real jolt to most individuals who participate. One architect said, "You can read about these problems in a textbook, but you can't really understand what the handicapped person is up against until you try to move around in a public building unassisted in a wheelchair."

Curb Cuts and Parking

Curb cuts for wheelchairs are making many city sidewalks accessible to wheelchairs. These sometimes increase the problems for the blind. One way to overcome this is using horizontal grooves to help those using canes to detect the curb. Another solution is a change in texture that is rougher than the sidewalk but less rough than the street. There is still much to be done to meet the needs of the varying types of handicapped.

Designated parking spaces for handicapped individuals are receiving wide attention. Many public buildings, parking lots, shopping centers, and others are making spaces available. But it's hard to keep thoughtless or uninformed people from usurping these spaces. Decals or stickers on cars indicating the handicapped person's right to park in them does help, but police and security guards still have a problem. More publicity to educate the general public is needed.

Radio and TV Programs

Some handicapped organizations are producing radio and TV programs offering information for the handicapped and also informing the public of the problems and achievements of the handicapped.

Many regular TV programs, news broadcasts, and others are beginning to include sign language interpreting as part of the program.

Service Centers

The Self-Dependence for the Handicapped Service Center, located at 25204 Mission Boulevard, Hayward, Calif., is operated by the Southern Alameda County chapter with the help of a $17,200 federal revenue sharing grant from the city of Hayward. The Center is the first of its kind to be run by the California Association for the Physically Handicapped.

Services offered by the Center include an attendant pool, a directory of accessible housing, help with employment, and workshops in self-help techniques. Some of the workshops are designed for the recently disabled and cover cooking from a wheelchair, getting in and out of cars, and applying for a transit discount card. Rap sessions are held every Wednesday evening, and peer counseling is available.

The Able–Disabled Advocacy Associates of San Diego, California, help ten handicapped men and women move from dependency on family or welfare to independent living each month. Federally funded in part by the Regional Employment and Training Consortium, Able–Disabled Advocacy sponsors MAINSTREAM magazine and its training program, Project HIRED for placement counseling and on-the-job training, and Access Survey—a project evaluating the accessibility of San Diego businesses.

Other communities have similar programs. Information is available from local handicapped organizations if you need the help offered or if you want to donate money to the program or participate in some other way.

Housing

Housing is still a major problem for many handicapped individuals. There are all kinds of programs being developed in different areas ranging from single family dwellings, apartment complexes built for the handicapped, existing houses or apartments remodeled, and mobile homes.

For information about housing facilities in your area, contact handicapped service centers, local handicapped associations, rehabilitation hospitals, or social services in your community.

The following three publications are of interest.

1. HOUSING AND HOME SERVICES FOR THE DISABLED, Gini Laurie
   Harper & Row, Pub., New York, N.Y.—Gini Laurie is one of the editors of REHABILITATION GAZETTE, which has been reporting developments in housing and services for the disabled since 1958 and in Independent Service Centers since 1972. The material on housing and independent living for the disabled is now compiled in this book.
2. ADAPTING MOBILE HOMES FOR USE BY THE HANDICAPPED
   Deborah Greenstein, Department of Housing and Urban Development, 451 7th Street SW, Room 8142, Washington, D.C. 20410—A $200,000 federal (HUD) research project on adapting mobile homes for use by the handicapped has recently been completed. Write to the address above for the free copy of the report. Applicable to any type of housing.
3. HOUSING FOR THE HANDICAPPED AND DISABLED, Marie McGuire Thompson
   National Association of Housing and Redevelopment, 2600 Virginia Avenue NW, Suite 404, Washington, D.C. 20037—The booklet has 176 pages on matching housing and specific handicaps, financing resources, selecting the right housing site, and resident oriented management and services.

Hopefully, the information in this book has offered solutions to some of your problems, given you a choice of options in many areas of your life, and helped expand your horizons by acquainting you with the lives of men and women who have achieved success and fulfillment in spite of overwhelming obstacles.

Adult education programs, 77-78
Advocacy centers, 207-8
Aid to Disabled (AID), 81-83
Aids to daily living, 7-19, 187-89
Air travel, 143-46
Alterations of clothing, 42-47
Appliances, kitchen, 63-64
Archery, 175-76
Art, 164
   career in, 91
Arthritis, stretch gloves for, 2-3
Automatic timers, 59

Baby blankets, 4
Baby plates, 11
Backrests, 3
Backscratcher, oriental, 4
Baking, 65
Baseball, 167
Basketball, 166-67
Basters, 64
Bath mitts, 8
Bathing aids, 8
Bathtub, cleaning of, 56
Bed supports, 3-4
Beep-ball games, 167
Bible, 197-98
   study groups, 200
Bicycle baskets for walkers, 13
Bicycling, 176
Bird watching and feeding, 160-61
Blankets, baby, 4
Blenders, 64
Books, 101-16
   braille, 115, 198
   cookbooks, 72-73
   large print, 114-15
   reading or listening to, 155-56
   rental cassettes of, 116
   on sex, 106-7
   talking, 115
   travel, 151-53
Bowling, 168-71
   equipment for, 170-71
   organizations for, 169-70
Braille books, 115
   Bibles, 198
Bras, sources for, 24
Brass rubbings, 158-59
Bread holders, 64
Breads, 65
   freezing, 70
Broilers, counter-top, 63
Brooms:
   electric, 56
   toy, 54, 56
Bulletin boards, 57
Burn remedies, 71
Business expenses, tax deductions for, 130
Bus travel, 148-49
Buying in bulk, 71

Caddies:
   cleaning, 60
   luggage, 154
Camper, travel by, 149
Camping, 179-80
Can openers, electric, 64

Canes:
   brightening of, 48-49
   places to stand, 57
Cannisters, 67
Cars:
   rentals of, 146
   travel by, 149
Careers, new, 89-96
Carpet sweepers, toy, 55
Cassettes, books on, 116
Castors, 57
Ceramics, 158
Charter airlines, 146
Children, books and booklets for, 101-2
Christian volunteer group, 201
Churches, 198-99
   accessible, 202, 205
Citizen band radios (CBs), 162-63
Cleaning caddies, soft-drink cartons **as**, 60
Cleaning tools, substitute, 54-56
Clean-up chores, kitchen, 66-67
Clothing, 20-52
   alterations and sewing of, 42-48
   care of, 51-52
   choice of, 49-51
   consultants on, 49
   kits for, 26-38
   for mastectomy patients, 38-42
   sources for, 20-42
Cold-water detergents, 58
Collecting, 156-57
Colleges:
   four-year, 80-81
   two-year, 78-80
Consultants, clothing, 49
Cooking, 62-75
   appliances, 63-64
   books, 72-73
   products, 74-75
   tips for, 67-70
   utensils and tools, 63-64
Corporate training programs, 84-85
Correspondence courses, 85-88
Crafts, 157-59
Crocheting, 159
Crutches, brightening of, 48-49
Cultural activities, 183-84
Curb cutting, 206-7
Cutting boards, 11

Deductions, income tax, 129-30
Dentist, career as, 90
Dentures, cleaning of, 8-9
Deodorants, 9
Department stores, substitute cleaning tools from, 55-56
Desserts, 65
Detergents, cold-water, 58
Dish mops, small, 55, 56
Dishwashing, 66-67
Doctor, career as, 90
Dogs, hearing-ear, 121
Dresses:
   back-opening, 21
   sources for, 23, 25
Dressing, aids to, 10-11
Drinking, aids to, 11-12
Drive-in churches, 199
Drop shelves, 62

Dryers, 64
Dusting, 56
Dustmop, child's, 54

Eating aids to, 11-12
Education, 76-88
  adult, 77-78
  corporate training programs, 84-85
  financial assistance for, 81
  four-year colleges, 80-81
  high school, 76-77
  home study, 85-88
  two-year college, 78-80
  vocational, 84
Egg beaters, 64
Egg slicers, 64
Eggs:
  boiling, 69
  one-handed breaking of, 70
Electronics, career in, 94
Employment assistance, federal and state programs for, 95-96
Engineer, career as, 92
Equipment, loan or rental of, 129

Fabric protector, 60
Financial assistance for education, 81-83
Fishing, 180
Flashlight, rechargeable pocket, 154
Flour shakers, 69
Foil dishes, disposable, 70
Foot supports, 3
Foreign-language health care guide, 142-143
Frozen desserts, 69
Fruit, fresh, 65

Games, 181
Gardening, 160
Garlic press, 64
Gelatin salads and desserts, 68
Girdles, sources for, 24
Golf, 174
Government jobs, 94
Grater plates, 64
Grills, electric, 63
Grooming aids, 9

Hair care, aids to, 9
Half sheet, satin, 4
Ham radio, 162, 163
Hand vacuums, 56
Health care:
  careers in, 94
  foreign-language guide, 142-43
Hearing-ear dogs, sources for, 121
Heating pad, cordless, 153
High school diploma, 76-77
Hobbies, 155-65
  art, 164
  bird watching and feeding, 160-61
  collecting, 156-57
  crafts, 157-59
  gardening, 160
  ham rado, CB and shortwave, 162-63
  music, 157
  needlework, sewing, crocheting, and knitting, 159
  pen or tape pals, 163-64
  photography, 161-62
  reading, 155-65
  writing, 164-65

Hockey, 174-75
Home business, career in, 93
Home improvements, tax deductions for, 129-30
Home study courses, 85-88
Homebound book services, 115
Horseback riding, 177
  career in training and, 92-93
Hotels:
  accessibility to, 205
  guides to, 150
Housework, 53-61
  hints for, 56-60
  organizing, 53-54
  substitute cleaning tools for, 54-56
Housing, 208
  alternatives, 131-132
Hunting, 180-81
Hypnotist, career as, 90

Ice hockey, 174-75
Income tax deductions, 129-30
Indoor gardening, 160
Inspirational publications, 107-14, 200-201
Insurance, 132
Ironing board
  other uses for, 55
  travel, 12

Kitchen:
  adaptions, 62-63
  clean-up chores in, 66-67
  See also Cooking
Kits, clothing, 26-38
Knife, electric, 64
Knitting, 159

Lamp bases, cleaning, 58-59
Large print books and magazines, 114-15, 197
Laundry:
  mini-, 154
  tips for, 60
Lawyer, career as, 89-90
Lazy susans, 12, 71
Leathercraft, 159
Library outreach services, 116
Listening to books, 155-56
Loans:
  of equipment, 129
  small business, 131
Luggage caddy, 154
Luminous paint and tape, 59

Macrame, 158
Magazines, 99-100
  large print, 114
Mail-order shopping, 133-36
Main dishes, 65
Make-up aids, 9
Mastectomy patients, clothing and products for, 38-42
Matchbook collecting, 156
Mechanic, career as, 92
Medical assistance on trip, 142
Medical expenses, tax deductions for, 130
Medical preparations for travel, 141-42
Menu planning, 65
Microwave ovens, 63
Mini-laundry, 154
Mixer, electric, 68
  portable, 64

Mixes, 70
Mixing bowls, 64
Mobile homes, 132
   travel by, 149
Money-saving, miscellaneous tips for, 136-37
Motels:
   accessibility to, 205   guides, 150
Motivational books, 107-14
Music, 157

Napkin holder, other uses for, 72
Needlework, 159
Newsletters, 100-101
Newspapers, large print, 100
Nightgowns, sources for, 26
Nonskid strips or flowers, 8, 12
Nylon net, 56

Oiling of kitchen tools, 69
Oral hygiene aids, 8-9
Organizations, 117-27
   assistance from, 129
   bowling, 169-70
   camping, 180
Outdoor gardening, 160

Packing tips, 140-41
Pamphlets:
   inspirational, 107-14, 200-201
   travel, 151-153
Pantsuits, sources for, 26
Paper grocery bags, 69
Paper products, 57
Parking, 206-7
Pen pal clubs, 163-64
Phone rest, shoulder, 12
Photography, 161-62
Piano keys, cleaning, 58
Pillows, versatile tailor-made, 2
Pizza rollers, 67
Plastic bags, 71
Plastic containers, 59
Plastic tumblers, 11-12
Pocket valise, 153
Pots and pans, storage of, 70
Prayer help by telephone, 200
Pressure, relief of, 1-2
Products for comfort, sources for, 4-6
Prostheses, breast, 38, 39, 42
Prosthesis technician, career as, 92
Public assistance, 128
Pull-out boards, 63
Puzzles, 181

Radio programs, 207
   religious, 199-200
Reading, 155-56
   See also Books
Recreational products, sources for, 184-86
Refrigerators, 64
Rehabilitation Act (1973), 90
Rental:
   of book cassettes, 116
   of cars, 146
Religious programs:
   radio, 199-200
   television, 200
Robes, back-opening, 21

Schools:
   accessible, 205
   See also Education
Secretary's chair, 63
Sewing, 42-48
   as hobby, 159
   tips for, 47-48
Sewing machines, 55
Sex, books on, 106-7
Shampoo, 9
Shaving, aids to, 9
Sheets, satin, 4, 13
Shelf linings, 57-58
Shoes, putting on, 11
Shortwave radios, 162, **163**
Shower hoods, vinyl, 8
Sightseeing, 181-83
   See also Travel
Sinks, 62
Skiiing, 172-74
Skillets
   electric, 63
   tri-section, 69
Slips, 10
   sources for, 24, 26
Small business loans, 131
Soap:
   holders for, 12-13
   preventing dropping of, 8
Social Security Disability, **128**
Socks:
   putting on, 10-11
   work, 4
Spatter lids, 68
Spiral binding for books, 13
Spiritual activities, 197-202
Sponge mops, 57
Sponge rubber, 1-2
Sponges as soap dishes, 59
Sport shirts, 10
Sports, 166-79
Spray cleaners, 56-58
Square dancing, wheelchair, **177**
Starch, laundry, 60
Stores, accessibility to, 205
Stoves, 63
Straws, extra-long, 11
Stretch gloves, 2-3
Supermarket, substitute cleaning tools from, **55**
Swimming, 171-72

Table tennis, 167
Table setting, 65-66
Talking books, 115
Tape pal clubs, 163-64
Teacher, career as, 91-92
Telephone:
   cleaning of, 58
   prayer help and inspiration by, 200
   shoulder rest for, 12
   tips for, 59
Tennis, 167
Thermal mugs, 4
Thimbles, 70
Toaster covers, **71**
Toothbrushes:
   cordless electric, 8
   other uses for, 58

"Top cleaning," 57
Towel, anchoring of, 8
Toy counter, substitute cleaning tools from, 54-55
Trade and technical schools, 84
Train travel, 147
Transporation, 203-4
Travel, 138-54
 air, 143-46
 books and pamphlets, 151-53
 bus, 148-49
 by car, camper, van or motor home, 149
 car rentals for, 146
 gadgets for, 153-54
 hotel/motel guides, 150
 medical assistance during, 142
 medical preparations for, 141-42
 packing for, 140-41
 special preparations for, 140
 train, 147
Travel agencies, 138-40
Travel organizer, 153
Tri-section skillets, 69
Trousers, putting on, 10-11
TV programs, 207
 religious, 200
Two-year colleges, 78-80

Universal travel adaptor, 153
Utensil holders, magnetized, 71
Utensils, kitchen, 63-64

Vacuuming, 56
Valise, pocket, 153
Van, travel by, 149
Vegetable brushes, 55
Vegetable peelers, 64
Vegetable tongs, 55
Vegetables, fresh, 65
Velcro fastenings, 10, 12
Veterans benefits, 130-31
Vocational training, 84
Voluntary organizations, assistance from, 129

Waffle irons, electric, 63
Walkers, bicycle basket for, 13
Wallpaper as shelf lining, 59
Wastebaskets, flip-top plastic, 58
Wheelchair basketball, 166-67
Wheelchair games, 177-79
Wheelchair squaredancing, 177
Wheelchairs:
 with CBs, 163
 brightening of, 48-49
 shirts for, 20-21
Whisks, 64
Wigs, 9
Woks, electric, 64
Wool sacks, 4
Woodwork, cleaning of, 58
Writing, career in:
 career in, 90-91
 as hobby, 164-165

Yardsticks
 magnet attached to, 72
 other uses of, 55

Zippers, 10